LEADING THE LAUNCH

A Ten-Stage Process for Successful District Initiatives

KIM WALLACE

Solution Tree | Press

Copyright © 2022 by Solution Tree Press

Materials appearing here are copyrighted. With one exception, all rights are reserved. Readers may reproduce only those pages marked "Reproducible." Otherwise, no part of this book may be reproduced or transmitted in any form or by any means (electronic, photocopying, recording, or otherwise) without prior written permission of the publisher.

555 North Morton Street
Bloomington, IN 47404
800.733.6786 (toll free) / 812.336.7700
FAX: 812.336.7790
email: info@SolutionTree.com
SolutionTree.com

Visit **go.SolutionTree.com/leadership** to download the free reproducibles in this book.

Printed in the United States of America

Library of Congress Cataloging-in-Publication Data

Names: Wallace, Kim, author.
Title: Leading the launch : a ten-stage process for successful district
   initiatives / Kim Wallace.
Description: Bloomington, IN : Solution Tree Press, 2021. | Includes
   bibliographical references and index.
Identifiers: LCCN 2021030196 (print) | LCCN 2021030197 (ebook) | ISBN
   9781952812699 (paperback) | ISBN 9781952812705 (ebook)
Subjects: LCSH: School districts--United States--Administration. |
   Educational leadership--United States. | Educational change--United
   States.
Classification: LCC LB2817.3 .W35 2021 (print) | LCC LB2817.3 (ebook) |
   DDC 379.1/535--dc23
LC record available at https://lccn.loc.gov/2021030196
LC ebook record available at https://lccn.loc.gov/2021030197

Solution Tree
Jeffrey C. Jones, CEO
Edmund M. Ackerman, President

Solution Tree Press
President and Publisher: Douglas M. Rife
Associate Publisher: Sarah Payne-Mills
Art Director: Rian Anderson
Managing Production Editor: Kendra Slayton
Copy Chief: Jessi Finn
Senior Production Editor: Christine Hood
Content Development Specialist: Amy Rubenstein
Proofreader: Evie Madsen
Text Designer: Laura Cox
Cover Designer: Rian Anderson
Editorial Assistants: Sarah Ludwig and Elijah Oates

Acknowledgments

This book is dedicated to my small and mighty family of three: my unwavering partner in love and life, MKB, and our spunky one-eyed terrier, Stella G. In their own unique ways, each kept me grounded, inspired, and energized throughout the writing and publication process. A special thanks goes to Marilyn for coining the term "process makes perfect," which constantly reminded me to persevere, persist, and prevail.

Solution Tree Press would like to thank the following reviewers:

Michael T. Adamson
Director of Board Services
Indiana School Boards Association
Indianapolis, Indiana

Tom Dodd
Principal
Lesher Middle School
Fort Collins, Colorado

Charles Ames Fischer
Educational Consultant
Decatur, Tennessee

Chris Hansen
Director of Learning
Hortonville Area School District
Greenville, Wisconsin

Josh Kunnath
English Teacher and Department Chair
Highland High School
Bakersfield, California

Philip D. Lanoue
Former Superintendent
Clarke County School District
Athens, Georgia

Erin Lawson
Principal
Little Harbour Elementary
Portsmouth, New Hampshire

Steven Weber
Associate Superintendent for Teaching and Learning
Fayetteville Public Schools
Fayetteville, Arkansas

Visit **go.SolutionTree.com/leadership** to download the free reproducibles in this book.

Table of Contents

Reproducibles are in italics.

About the Author	ix
Introduction	1
The Ins and Outs of Implementation	2
Barriers to Implementation	5
In This Book	7
Introduction Action Plan: Checklist	8

1 Stage 1: Research and Vet the Idea 9
   The Leadership Team 11
   Six Steps for Vetting the Idea 12
   Conclusion 18
   Stage 1 Action Plan: Checklist and Reproducible 18
   Initiative Vetting Notetaking Tool *19*

2 Stage 2: Pitch the Proposal 21
   Tuning Protocol 21
   Two Real-World Scenarios 24
   Conclusion 33
   Stage 2 Action Plan: Checklist and Reproducible 33
   Protocol-Planning Template *34*

3 Stage 3: Determine Priorities 37
   Initiative Overload 37
   Criteria for Preventing Initiative Overload 39
   Conclusion 51
   Stage 3 Action Plan: Checklist and Reproducibles 51
   Initiative Prioritization Rubric *52*
   District Plans Crosswalk *55*
   Cost-Benefit Analysis *56*

4 Stage 4: Design the Proof of Concept, Prototype, and Pilot . . . 57
Blueprint for Action 58
Conclusion 64
Stage 4 Action Plan: Checklist and Reproducibles 65
Four Critical Questions for the Pilot 66
Mid-Pilot Process Check 67

5 Stage 5: Build Stakeholder Engagement 69
Stakeholder Groups 69
The Cs of Communication 71
A Plan for Outreach 72
One Size Does Not Fit All 75
Conclusion 78
Stage 5 Action Plan: Checklist and Reproducibles 79
Stakeholder Groups 80
Maslow's Hierarchy of Needs Analysis 83

6 Stage 6: Gather and Analyze Data 85
Surveys 86
Focus Groups 91
Supplemental Data Compilation Methods 94
Conclusion 96
Stage 6 Action Plan: Checklist and Reproducibles 96
Survey Mapping Tool 97
Focus Group Mapping Tool 98
Data Analysis Form 99

7 Stage 7: Make a Decision 101
Green Light, Yellow Light, or Red Light 101
The Art and Science of Decision Making 108
Conclusion 109
Stage 7 Action Plan: Checklist and Reproducibles 109
Questions and Commitments Notetaking Tool 110
Decision-Making Rubric 111
Team Decision-Making Assessment 112
Criteria for Green-Lighting, Yellow-Lighting, or Red-Lighting an Initiative 114

8 Stage 8: Plan and Deliver Professional Development 115
Key Features of Effective Professional Development 115
Agenda Design 120
Professional Development Sustained Delivery 120
Conclusion 121
Stage 8 Action Plan: Checklist and Reproducibles 124
Professional Development Design Worksheet 125
Agenda-Planning Form 128

9   Stage 9: Implement the Initiative **129**
Assessment and Accountability 130
Three Scenarios of Best-Laid Plans 133
How to Move Forward 135
Conclusion 138
Stage 9 Action Plan: Checklist and Reproducibles 139
Self-Assessment and Rating Scale Continuum *140*
Implementation Observation Tool *141*
Stakeholder Representative Assignments *142*

10   Stage 10: Provide Ongoing Support **143**
A Culture of Continued Growth 144
Assistance and Support 148
Unproductive Practices 149
Conclusion 152
Stage 10 Action Plan: Checklist and Reproducibles 152
Steering Guide for Monitoring Progress *153*
Initiative Assessment Tool *154*

Epilogue: Balancing Acts **155**
Three Categories for Implementation 155
Three Orders of Barriers to Change 157
Epilogue Action Plan: Checklist and Reproducible 159
Initiative Implementation Process: Guidance Document *160*

References and Resources **163**

Index **167**

About the Author

**Kim Wallace, EdD,** is a professional educational consultant with Process Makes Perfect, a company that specializes in developing real-world solutions for educators. She consults, writes, and presents nationally on the topics of 21st century leadership, curriculum and instruction, organizational change, and future trends in education. She also works at the University of California, Berkeley, overseeing a statewide center that provides coaching and support to K–12 administrators and aspiring teacher leaders.

Kim began her career as a twenty-two-year-old high school English and social science teacher at her alma mater, Castro Valley High School, in the San Francisco East Bay (where her parents met as high school teachers themselves). She eventually shifted into site and district administration, hoping to make a larger impact on student learning. She served in a K–12 leadership position as the superintendent of one of the top-twenty largest school districts in California. After twenty-six years as a public educator, Kim decided to branch into higher education to assist graduate schools of education and leadership preparation programs with designing and delivering more relevant and authentic learning experiences for practitioners out in the field.

For her innovative work as an assistant superintendent of instruction, the Association of California School Administrators (ACSA) recognized Kim in 2015 as the Region 6 Administrator of the Year for Curriculum and Instruction. Kim also received an Excellence in Education Award as Davis Joint Unified School District's Administrator of the Year from the Yolo County School Boards Association in 2014. On the national platform, she has been invited to deliver several keynote addresses and regularly conducts interactive workshops, such as at the Association for Supervision and

Curriculum Development (ASCD) Leadership Summit and RTM K–12 National Superintendents Forum.

Kim earned a bachelor's degree in history at the University of California, Santa Barbara. She earned her master's degree in education at the University of California, Los Angeles, and finally culminated her educational goals with a doctorate in education from the University of California, Davis.

To learn more about Kim's work, visit Process Makes Perfect (https://processmakesperfect.org).

To book Kim Wallace for professional development, contact pd@SolutionTree.com.

Introduction

There is no institution more noble or essential to our collective well-being as a society than K–12 education. And the educators within are the inventors, innovators, guardians, champions, and challengers of convention. We are the quintessential optimists hoping for a better future. That hope, when coupled with purposeful intention and strategic action, levels the playing field for progress toward increased equity, social justice, and economic welfare for all.

This is not Sir Thomas More's *Utopia* (1972), devoid of conflict, struggle, or dissension; rather, it's an experiment by which we constantly strive for improvement, achievement, and success. That continual effort is taking place in classrooms, teachers' lounges, principals' offices, district board rooms, families' kitchen tables, and virtual environments. In many ways, we are connected like never before, peering into a future so many of us desire to harness, design, and transform into new ways of living, learning, and working. Much like the birth of widespread public education in the 19th century, we are experiencing a unique and precious opportunity for a rebirth of our cherished educational system to improve the lives of today's and tomorrow's children as well as the world they will inherit.

One of the most common shared experiences around the world is going to school. We learned to color between the lines. In some cultures, we are trained to stand still and wait our turn. We memorize the multiplication tables. We sing the alphabet song and take spelling tests. We eat bagged lunches from home and tater tots in the cafeteria and play hopscotch or other games at recess. We are told to raise our hands before speaking. Many of our childhood memories and stories last with us forever.

Schools everywhere are profoundly embedded in our collective fabric. It's not an exaggeration to proclaim that we've all done school in certain ways pretty much forever. And for those of us who have chosen to *do school* as a profession, we're faced with upholding revered customs while also spearheading transformation to move society forward. Most educators, by nature, have generous hearts, inquisitive minds, and active hands. Most of us have chosen the profession (or the profession has chosen us) because we deeply care about the future and want to contribute to the betterment of society.

THE INS AND OUTS OF IMPLEMENTATION

Anyone who has worked in the field of education for more than a few years has seen myriad initiatives come and go. As district office or site leadership changes, teachers often brace themselves for some fresh "flavor of the month" while waiting for "this too, to pass." Though this recurring cycle may feel somewhat inevitable—as leaders have differing visions, passions, and philosophies—what does *not* have to be inevitable is the process by which initiatives are introduced and infused into school or district.

Each new school year, the system bursts with promising projects, pilots, propositions, programs, personnel, plans, plots, platforms, procedures, and policies. Integrating these innovations into the curriculum requires a substantial amount of effort—pedagogically, physically, and psychologically—and school conditions for making these changes are not always the best. Protecting the status quo is not always intentional, but challenging it takes courage.

It is from these optimistic mindsets and orientations that education leaders generate ideas and plans to improve student learning and well-being. Good intentions, however, are not enough. We can want what's best, but if we forsake the necessary planning, there are no guarantees. There are many practical and philosophical questions to answer in our attempts to successfully launch a new initiative. By instilling a process to vet potential proposals, we can filter through the *just OK* and *good* ideas and get to the *great* ones. It's really all about implementation.

To help you further understand the definition of *implementation* in contrast to other ways an initiative might filter throughout a school or district, Aaron Lyon (2017) delineates the following nuances:

> Implementation can be thought about in comparison to other ways that innovations spread in organizations. Diffusion refers to passive, unplanned, and untargeted spread of information or interventions. Dissemination refers to targeted distribution of information and intervention materials to a specific audience. Dissemination activities typically focus on improving a practice or policy audience's knowledge and awareness. However, dissemination is not enough to change professional behavior. In contrast, implementation means using deliberate strategies in specific settings to adopt new interventions, integrate them effectively, and change practice patterns. (p. 1)

The concepts of *dissemination* and *diffusion* as nonexemplars shine a light on the deliberateness of the verb *to implement*. While the previous two terms may have some agency and consciousness involved, the latter has a more active purpose behind changing behaviors. Furthermore, the word *implement* can be used as a noun or verb. As a noun, *implement* means a "tool, utensil, or other piece of equipment, especially as used for a particular purpose" (Lexico, n.d.). As a verb, *implement* means "to put a decision, plan, or agreement into effect" (Lexico, n.d.). Both definitions are essential to executing an initiative. One must have the right *tools* in place to hit the targets for *action*.

But first, let's take a look at what constitutes a new initiative. The term *new* can actually involve a combination of scenarios. It might be something that:

- Has never been done before
- Has been tried in the past, but not for many years
- Currently exists, but significant changes are being considered
- Is widespread, large scale, or will affect many stakeholders
- Requires resources above and beyond what is currently budgeted or planned for (human resources, materials, professional development, time, funding)

How long should all of this take? It depends. Smaller initiatives could be completed within a few months, while larger ones might be a year or longer. Since some stages take longer than others, depending on the circumstances, the adage *go slow to go fast* should drive the timeline.

This practical guide sets forth a course of action to implement new initiatives effectively into schools and districts that will stand the test of time. School leaders and district office administrators alike will benefit from learning ways to break through existing barriers, vet potential ideas, and create strategic plans for the effective execution of innovative tools, programs, or protocols in service to students. Initiatives can range from instructional endeavors, such as infusing college and career readiness into the core curriculum or altering a middle school schedule to allow for science, technology, engineering, art, and math (STEAM) opportunities, to an institutional change in practice or process, such as adopting a new student information system or districtwide discipline policy. Establishing a set of checks and balances for new initiatives not only streamlines the implementation but also results in a higher-quality product, program, or practice.

Employing realistic case studies, examples, and scenarios to connect to familiar experiences, I pose solutions to common dilemmas and offer procedural approaches to overcome challenges. You will gain a deeper understanding of change management theory, learn research-based methods to address challenges, and acquire practical templates, models, and frameworks for immediate use in your school.

This book outlines a protocol consisting of ten stages to successfully implement new initiatives. The first three stages include researching and vetting the idea, pitching the proposal, and determining priorities. Curiosity, inquiry, and study dominate this stage. Sentence starters like, "What if we . . . ," "How might we . . . ," and "Can we consider . . ." prompt open-ended thinking about the topic at hand. This is the laboratory where many ideas fail to thrive—and that's a good thing. We want only the potentially fittest to survive.

The next three stages involve testing out the proof of concept through designing a prototype and piloting it on a limited scale. Once the pilot period is underway, the leadership team solicits feedback from stakeholders and collects data for analysis. The team should employ multiple measures to reduce the potential for a biased outcome that doesn't authentically reflect the true pros and cons of the initiative.

Then it's decision-making time. After presenting the findings, the leadership team collectively decides to green-light, yellow-light, or red-light the project. While yellow-lighting and red-lighting may kick the initiative back to an earlier stage or stop it in its tracks, respectively, a green-lighted initiative will proceed to the final stages in the process to bolster success. Professional development, clear and frequent communication, and ongoing support will help embed the fledgling initiative into practice. Figure I.1 shows an overview of the ten-stage process.

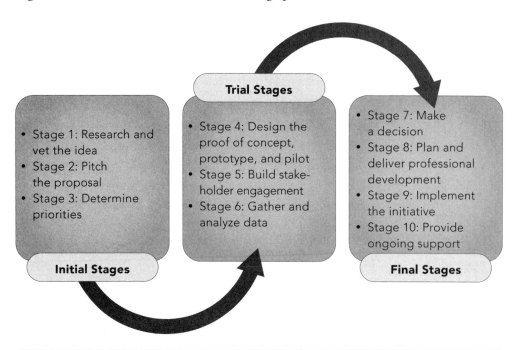

Figure I.1: Ten stages of the initiative implementation process.

Before even entertaining a new initiative, one should examine the motivation for doing so. Sometimes it's plainly a mandate such as the following.

- Legislation stipulates that all school districts add an ethnic studies course to their high school graduation requirements.
- A civil rights lawsuit is settled by requiring all staff to be trained in gender spectrum awareness.
- The curriculum and instruction department must institute new state-adopted social science resources to meet the 2011 Fair, Accurate, Inclusive, and Respectful (FAIR) Education Act.

In other situations, a district or state may impose an initiative from the outside, such as sanctions being levied on a district by the state's department of education for persistently low student achievement scores or having an unbalanced budget. Addressing these situations is not optional and, although they may have a different kind of pressure and intensity, leadership teams can approach them similarly to an elected initiative.

Intrinsically driven motives, on the other hand, may include voluntarily and willingly enhancing or altering programs or services for students and staff. For example:

- To cut costs, the technology advisory committee is recommending going from three separate yet overlapping communication services down to one.
- The elementary-level Spanish dual immersion program is spread across the district and would like to consolidate at a single site instead.
- The district's student support services department is interested in moving from site-based paper forms to centralized online enrollment.

All these initiatives are worthy pursuits, even if not compulsory. Whether the arena is a school site or district office, the options we select will have a long-lasting effect. The initiatives inherited from our predecessors are a bit of a different animal than those we develop from scratch, however. Sometimes intervention is the operating system needed when stepping into an initiative already underway. When crafting one's own initiatives, however, many pitfalls can be avoided by following a series of preplanned stages.

BARRIERS TO IMPLEMENTATION

The precursor to getting started is first untangling the roots of why educational initiatives can flounder in the first place. There are deep undercurrents related to the adoption of new products and practices in the field of education. Peggy Ertmer (1999), identifies two orders of barriers to technology integration in the classroom: (1) *first-order barriers*—equipment, resources, and support and (2) *second-order barriers*—knowledge, skills, beliefs, and attitudes. While Ertmer (1999) developed this theory specifically to technological adoptions, we can broaden and apply it to new initiatives requiring shifts in materials, mindsets, and organizational culture. Although this theory is dated and technology has advanced exponentially since 1999, it still holds true.

First-order barriers may include procuring external resources (for example, adequate numbers of devices, consumables, professional development, coaching, or technical support), while second-order barriers present intrinsic obstacles to effective integration (for example, opinions, feelings, past experiences, and perceptions). These two barriers can be focused down to *skill* and *will*—just as has been widely applied to research on teacher efficacy and student learning. *Skill* is akin to knowing how to do something and being able to do it well, while *will* is about one's attitude toward learning. When students are faced with new tasks or concepts and exhibit resistance, it can be helpful to find out if skill, will, or both are in play. Adults, likewise, bring their own unique and varying levels of openness to new concepts as well as abilities to adapt their former routines into novel approaches. In 2005, Ertmer expanded on her research by noting: "Three strategies seem to hold particular promise for promoting change in teacher beliefs about teaching and learning, in general, and beliefs about technology, specifically: (a) personal experiences, (b) vicarious experiences, and (c) social-cultural influences" (p. 32). These aspects also influence educators' receptiveness and affinity to new initiatives as well.

Robyn Jackson (2013) developed several tools to illustrate how skill and will intersect, one of which is displayed in table I.1.

Table I.1: Skill or Will

Teacher Type	Characteristics	Looks Like
Low Skill and High Will	Enthusiastic; idealistic; unwilling to learn	Seeks feedback and explores new strategies and ideas, but implementation is inconsistent and ineffective
Low Skill and Low Will	Discouraged; not invested; "retired on the job"	Does not volunteer or contribute; passive; tries to stay beneath the radar
High Skill and High Will	Motivated and skillful	Easily identifies and implements appropriate strategies; explores new ideas, seeks feedback, and refines practice; takes on challenges
High Skill and Low Will	Skillful but disinterested; "has seen it all"	Unreceptive to feedback; resists efforts to try new approaches; saboteur

Source: Jackson, 2013, p. 15.

First- and second-order barriers don't exist in a vacuum, but rather within a school or district's context, culture, and history. Then there are third-order barriers. *Third-order barriers* (for example, pressure to cover the curriculum or teach to the test, fixed bell schedules, negotiated labor contracts, or parent or community expectations) can create additional hurdles (Wallace, 2012). While teachers and administrators often have some locus of control over first- and second-order barriers, third-order barriers can transcend their influence. Furthermore, the environment itself may need to change or an otherwise fruitful endeavor may wither on the vine. Mastering first-, second-, and third-order barriers requires a conscious knowledge that change management is the driver and that the road ahead has many curves.

IN THIS BOOK

This book will walk you through the ten stages of the initiative implementation process. Chapters 1, 2, and 3 outline the initial stages of researching and vetting, developing and pitching the proposal, and determining its placement and prioritization in the overall scheme of a school or district. Chapters 4, 5, and 6 contain the key ingredients for designing the proof of concept, prototype, and pilot; building stakeholder engagement; and gathering and analyzing data.

After the first six stages of the new initiative process are complete, chapter 7 tackles the "to be or not to be" culminating decision to push the plan forward, slow it down, or shelve it. Once a proposal is approved, the final three stages are put into motion. Chapter 8 attends to the clear communication of professional development plans prior to the actual implementation process, which is outlined in chapter 9, and its need for ongoing support, outlined in chapter 10. To help districts and schools balance and sustain their most impactful initiatives, the epilogue delves into eliminating ineffective and outdated programs to make room for systemwide growth and concludes with a summary of the ten-stage process.

Although the upcoming chapters describe the ten stages sequentially, they are not meant to be lockstep or set in stone. If we've learned anything in our collective years as educators, it's that very little is ever completely predictable, and the ability to pivot to respond to evolving times and changing conditions is paramount to progress. You may choose to combine certain phases or execute them simultaneously depending on different variables or conditions in your own unique environment. The leadership charge in front of us calls for ingenuity, teamwork, responsiveness, and flexibility. But most of all—passion.

Perfection is a process, not a destination. One initiative at a time.

Educators can use this guide in a myriad of ways. It's ideal for a team book study or a handbook for administrators to help them advance their schools and districts to the next level. It includes strategies, tools, examples, and case studies throughout to help you at each stage of the process.

Finally, to help you organize and hit the benchmarks throughout the process, the end of each chapter presents an action plan with a checklist, reproducibles, or both to guide and document the work toward your specific initiative. It's a great way to track your progress in a snapshot and communicate the level of thoughtfulness and due diligence the team exerts to bring this important program, policy, process, or practice to life in your school or district.

Following is an overview of what's included in this book.

- **Process:** A set of procedures to lead to desired goals and outcomes in the new initiative implementation process
- **Case studies:** Hypothetical scenarios that illustrate the stages in the context of a variety of education settings
- **Stages:** Ten sequential stages containing the overarching ingredients to advance you through the implementation process via short-term discrete actions
- **Action plan checklists and reproducibles:** Models, templates, charts, and reproducibles to be adopted, adapted, or improved on for use in your own school or district, and help guide you through the process

INTRODUCTION ACTION PLAN: CHECKLIST

The following checklist helps you apply what you learned in the introduction and move forward to the first stage of the initiative implementation process.

☐ Define your new initiative in a few sentences (elevator pitch).

☐ Determine whether it is externally or internally initiated and how that may affect your approach.

☐ Examine and call out the three barrier levels that may exist in your school or district related to this implementation.

CHAPTER 1

Stage 1: Research and Vet the Idea

"**H**ey, I have an idea!" a principal, grade-level leader, department chair, director, or board member says. Your response: "Great! Let's launch the new initiative process!" But wait. Not so fast. Early stages in the process should not be rushed, as they are necessary to identify gaps and strengths in the fledgling proposition. By the time someone actually decides to float their idea to others, they have likely been incubating the notion internally for quite a while. While that individual may be well-versed in the research or rationale, others will need the chance to catch up.

This chapter walks you through the first stage of the initiative implementation process, which focuses on laying the groundwork for planning and building your initial coalition which later becomes a formal leadership team. Each section contains guiding questions for consideration, illustrative examples, and explanations about how the idea-scouting process unfolds. But the most important starting point is expanding the team's capacity by engaging with expert leaders, whether formally recognized as leaders or not.

Most leaders in the field of education started out as teachers. In the classroom, they have significant influence over their own domain. The students are *their* students; the lesson plans, *their* lessons. Personal choices and instructional decisions affect a limited number of people on a daily basis. A botched biology experiment, Socratic seminar, or history lecture during first period not only can be salvaged in second period but also perfected by the fourth. A first-grade class getting too rowdy during an art project can be corralled into quiet listeners on the carpet for story time in a matter of minutes. Simply put, teachers can nimbly shift directions when things aren't going as planned and make any needed course corrections. They do this expertly throughout each day. It is truly at the core of the art and science of teaching.

Many of these skillful teachers eventually seek site and district leadership roles because they believe they can improve the system, successfully manage people, create change, or bring about cultural shifts on a larger scale. These aspiring leaders want to take charge of a situation, school, or district and make it better; in the most noble of cases, on behalf of students. Creativity, innovation, and inspiration are hallmarks of top-tier administrators—it is the reason they get hired (and sometimes the reason they get fired). Trial and error between the four walls of a classroom is one thing. When overseeing a department, school site, or district office, however, the consequences can outlast even one's tenure.

What good leaders soon learn, if they are not already inherently wired that way, is that they cannot do it alone. Sheer will, skill, or drill will only move one's vision so far. In fact, it's the unique combination of big-picture thinking and attention-to-detail execution that yields results. And the good news is, a leader can be stronger in one arena than another if he or she builds a team that collectively covers each of those qualities and more. This team building should be done before the idea vetting even begins. Without a team and a rigorous protocol to vet ideas for large-scale implementation, leaders may be destined to repeat patterns of implementation and potentially overload the system, cultivate mistrust, take fatal missteps, or witness failure to launch.

In *Leading by Design: An Action Framework for PLC at Work Leaders*, Cassandra Erkens and Eric Twadell (2012) describe seven effective leadership practices to keep in mind as you delve into this first stage in the process.

1. **Creating and sustaining collaborative relationships:** Leadership teams can only thrive when functional, honest, and open relationships exist. Building authentic trust takes time, but it will pay off in the outcomes.

2. **Aligning systems:** The school system is not a single system but a complex web of several interactive habitats. Synchronicity occurs when there is consciousness and intention in alignment between the parts and the whole.

3. **Facilitating shared responsibility:** While an initiative may be the brainchild of one team member, he or she will need allies prior to launch. Truly securing buy-in means that others pledge to hold themselves just as responsible for its success as the initiator does.

4. **Building coherence and clarity:** This pairing is essential for pitching, explaining, and building momentum for a new idea. Often, in order to be comfortable with an initiative, stakeholders must first comprehend the *what*, *when*, *where*, *why*, and *how* behind it.

5. **Modeling practices and expectations:** Seeing is believing. A leadership team must exhibit the attributes they expect others to follow and set clear boundaries for what the implementation is and what it isn't.

6. **Reflecting on leadership effectiveness of self and others:** Humility is of the essence here. Every initiative, no matter how great the leader or the preplanning, will face unanticipated stumbling blocks. It's how we reflect on, own, and react to those challenges that matter most.
7. **Developing leadership capacity in self and others:** The beauty of true teamwork is the collective evolution in leadership resulting from the collaboration process. Listening, sharing, and being vulnerable with each other elevates the whole team.

Keep these attributes in mind as we delve into the deliberate composition of the team and the six steps in the vetting process that govern stage 1.

THE LEADERSHIP TEAM

Richard DuFour, Rebecca DuFour, Robert Eaker, Thomas W. Many, and Mike Mattos (2016) assert that in order for a group of people to work as a *team*, they must be "working together *to achieve a common goal* for which members are held mutually accountable" (page 91). The term *team* primarily refers to a full-time core group of leaders involved in a project; however, it may intermittently include part-time players who engage at certain relevant points in the process when teams desire their expertise or perspectives. For consistency and clarity, I may refer to the leadership team as *the team* unless I specify that it's a differently configured team, such as a decision-making team or consulting team. Regardless of the make-up, the emphasis DuFour and colleagues (2016) place on common goals and commitments to accountability are the key elements of teamwork.

As most major implementations originate at the central office or within a site instructional leadership team (ILT), administrators are typically the ones to construct their team. High-performing teams should be customized by role, perspective, and experience related to the specific initiative. The entire initiative implementation process hinges on robust team participation; therefore, careful thought must go into its development. For optimal productivity, the ideal team size is approximately six to ten members, although others may be consulted along the way for their expertise, research, data, or feedback. Each official team member will have his or her own departments or point people that he or she relies on to bounce ideas off of between meetings and shares those perspectives with the core team.

Whether the idea originated from grassroots origins out in the field or developed at the district office, an intentionally formed team shares responsibility for improving student outcomes as part of the systemwide improvement efforts. The team leader should be enthusiastic, committed for the long haul, and have the skills to effectively lead others. In evaluating what the implementation entails, the leader will then assemble a diverse team with the appropriate knowledge, expertise, and collaboration skills to support the first stage in the protocol. Teams should be comprised of thought leaders at the district level, hands-on site administrators, and others who will be directly impacted by the decision to drive the recommendation forward, such as teachers, classified staff, or students.

In addition to traditional titles or positions, the leader should also consider people who might serve in informal roles that can shed light on a new enterprise. For example, if the initiative calls for a significant change in custom, a person who is a cultural insider should be on board. That person has been in the school or district for a long time, is well respected by others, and knows the history of other attempts at initiatives. If the initiative is instructional in nature, one or more individuals with expert content knowledge and pedagogical strategies should be involved. This might be a highly-skilled classroom teacher, instructional coach, or content area program manager. An initiative that requires technical understanding or complex systems thinking should involve big-picture thinkers who can communicate complicated concepts clearly to a general audience. The overall goal is to develop a consortium with distinct views and aptitudes, so also select others who know something about finances, human resources, professional development, or community politics, or who have local business connections.

SIX STEPS FOR VETTING THE IDEA

Once a think tank of colleagues (who may or may not become the official leadership team) is assembled, the idea vetting process begins. This is not the place to shoot down the initiative before it even gets off the ground, but a time for open conversation about why the leader is bringing it forward. The leader sets up a meeting with consulting team members and guides them through a six-step discussion on the idea vetting process.

1. Identify the rationale or reason for developing the initiative.
2. Develop awareness and alignment around the proposal.
3. Tap into history and background.
4. Forecast the future.
5. Anticipate the impact on and reaction of stakeholders.
6. Brainstorm estimated costs.

IDENTIFY THE RATIONALE OR REASON FOR DEVELOPING THE INITIATIVE

Identifying the rationale immediately gets us closer to the core beliefs behind the initiative's purpose. As Simon Sinek (2011) asserts, successful leaders build out their ideas from the essential question of *why* we are here as an organization before moving on to the *how* and *what*. Starting with *why* causes the brain to pause, assess the underlying drive, and articulate the goal. Sometimes it is merely answering this question alone that stalls or spurs on the next steps in the process. A school district's mission and vision may provide a window into the goals and ideals that each new initiative should advance or enhance. Depending on the breadth, depth, and quality of the existing mission and vision, clear lines must be drawn between the potential implementation and the district's purpose for being.

Consider a school district that began noticing a trend in mental health incidents at the high schools in recent years. Frighteningly, this year, these incidents have increased in frequency not only in teenagers but are also showing up every other week at the middle and elementary schools. This high-achieving community, where parents and teachers emphasize academics above all else, may be contributing to the students' poor mental health, coping strategies, and self-care.

Noting the spike in calls that result in hospitalization, the principals urge the director of student support services to explore social-emotional learning (SEL) curriculum and stress management tools to use with their students. Instead of looking immediately for packaged programs or approaches, the director sits down with the principals to explore the reasons why they think students are increasingly struggling. The answer to that *why*, as well as the *why* behind what it means to educate the whole child, should better guide the district in finding solutions tailored to their particular student needs. This hypothetical scenario illustrates the starting point for launching the new initiative process. The leader becomes aware of a need, consults with colleagues to learn more about the situation, and formulates a plan to pursue solutions.

The *why*, followed by the *what* and *how*, establishes the fundamental infrastructure for the new initiative. The following guiding questions can help leadership teams going through this first step in the process.

GUIDING QUESTIONS

- Why is this initiative critical to our mission of educating students?
- What problem, issue, or concern are we seeking to solve?
- How will the project, product, or service enhance student learning?

DEVELOP AWARENESS AND ALIGNMENT AROUND THE PROPOSAL

In a country as diverse as the United States or Canada, what will resonate in one town or city may not in other regions. Demographics, such as race, ethnicity, education level, socioeconomics, landscape (rural, suburban, urban), language, culture, local industry or occupations, and religious or political affiliations, engender unique dynamics in every district. The city of Honolulu, Hawaii, has a very different flavor from Jackson, Mississippi; and Jackson is quite a distinctive community from Winnipeg, Canada.

Awareness of the local community's character and values can make way for a smoother implementation. That said, sometimes those attributes contradict laws and policies that are required to be enacted via the initiative. These controversial topics might include sexual health and puberty education, science instruction related to the origins of the universe, or literature with perceived objectionable moral content. Alignment with the community's culture and values means finding a mutual position of agreement or alliance on any given topic or initiative. Being in touch with, as well as validating, stakeholders' perspectives, experiences, beliefs, and opinions demonstrates respect and builds rapport with the community's interests.

Possessing awareness and creating alignment does not mean, however, that one must maintain the status quo. This is about knowing one's audience and *how* to approach the proposed change with regard to how in sync it will likely be within the community. All communities have hidden minefields—underlying issues or sacrosanct traditions that cannot be touched without setting off an explosion; in other words, it may not be worth the upheaval the initiative will cause if the team chooses to move forward. Incremental steps toward the goal or developing a variation on the theme may be an alternative method for implementation if the initiative is likely to be at odds with community cultures or values.

GUIDING QUESTIONS

- How does this initiative support our district's mission and vision?
- How does it align with our core values?
- What are the expectations of the school community: families, parents, and businesses?
- Does it require a shift in culture?
- Are any other districts doing something similar?

TAP INTO HISTORY AND BACKGROUND

The more things change, the more they *seem* to stay the same. Every district has a core group of people who have seen it all and possess historical knowledge of past initiatives just like the one in front of them. Tapping into this institutional memory will be of service to the present as well as the future. Inquiring about how implementation went the first time, what could have improved its success, or simply hearing perspectives that provide a framework can flesh out the new idea immensely.

If the initiative does indeed have predecessors, constructing a timeline can show the context of this initiative in relation to those from the past. Openly acknowledging the lessons learned from the first time around will reassure those who experienced it earlier on that the same mistakes will be avoided. Regardless of whether this initiative builds on a former model or if it's truly a fresh innovation in the district, people will often connect it to some schema in their mind that colors their perspective, positively or negatively. When a team brings those connections to light, it can address the issues directly, instead of letting them lurk dangerously in the shadows.

GUIDING QUESTIONS

- If there are related initiatives from the past, how successful were they?
- Is there any baggage to consider? False starts?
- How might we address earlier missteps?
- Where does the initiative fit within existing frameworks or strategic plans?

FORECAST THE FUTURE

While there is never a crystal ball to predict the outcome of any attempt, an eye on the future can help smooth the path. Scanning the horizon for potential effects of implementation means taking into consideration several facets, including political currents, job market trends, cutting-edge innovations, new media landscapes, generational shifts, and social perspectives. This is about anticipating needs that we can barely see. Before they bear down on us, however, we can often look for hints from students themselves.

Although it's tempting for adults to think they know better and approach things from a didactic standpoint, asking young people about their thoughts, feelings, hopes, and fears provides a glimpse into the future they are both inheriting and designing. A quote often attributed to Albert Einstein says, "We can't solve problems by using the same kind of thinking we used when we created them" (BrainyQuote, n.d.). This takes some humility on leaders' parts. Authentically listening to the people we are supposed to be serving may uncover uncomfortable truths and realities we aren't prepared to take on. But even if we don't pay heed, it doesn't make them go away.

Consider Greta Thunberg, the teen from Sweden who took the world by storm in 2019 demanding that leaders do something *now* about climate change (Encyclopaedia Britannica, 2021). Thunberg's tactic was to not only increase awareness but also ignite real action. Youth all over the world are maneuvering unconventionally as well to bring attention to other critical issues such as Black Lives Matter and gender equality, so it's critical that education leaders step outside their own paradigms. Therefore, widening the scope beyond one's current reality is paramount.

GUIDING QUESTIONS

- How does this initiative prepare students for the future?
- What is the impact on student learning today?
- What do you see this evolving into? What might be the long-term plan?

ANTICIPATE THE IMPACT ON AND REACTION OF STAKEHOLDERS

Schools are places where all of society is represented and gathers in a shared environment. Unlike the business world, the education sector is expected to serve everyone, including students with special needs, English learners, homeless and foster youth, and every religion, ethnicity, and orientation—high and low performers alike. Some initiatives might focus on enhancing services for one particular student group, while others may address all students. Identifying stakeholders is key. Once you know whom the initiative addresses, reach out and get their feedback on the proposed change, as it will have a direct impact on them. If the goal is improved learning, we should always check in with the students.

The other players might include administrators, teachers, employee groups, parents, the local community, the school district's board of trustees, and other district office departments such as human resources, business services, or instructional services. Getting everyone to agree on what's right for students is a tall order. The goal here is not getting everyone to agree, however, but to anticipate potential reactions and manage them as best as you can. Strong opposition from any stakeholders can sink a proposal. So it's critical to step into the shoes of others while considering an initiative and then craft a plan to reach out to them with the appropriate tools.

For example, if you are introducing a new paradigm, such as the Next Generation Science Standards (NGSS; NGSS Lead States, 2013), enlisting trusted teachers to share the shifts with a skeptical parent group who feel that the existing way of teaching science should stay intact can be effective. Initiatives related to certificated staff, such as teachers and counselors, may require some groundwork with the leaders of their unions or associations. The superintendent writing a joint memo with the president of the union sharing support for and commitment to a new program builds trust and unity. When the initiative requires additional work from already busy site administrators, spending some time in a principals' meeting gathering input to lighten their load shows district office support. The bottom line is clear—ongoing communication is a two-way street.

GUIDING QUESTIONS

- What are the best possible ways to reach different stakeholders?
- How can we involve students in the process?
- What strategies will we use to develop allies early on to support the initiative?
- How will we address opposition?
- Are there contractual implications that we may need to negotiate with employee associations or labor unions?

BRAINSTORM ESTIMATED COSTS

Money talks . . . and walks. It's critically important to discover up front whether your district has the budget to both fund the purchase and upkeep; and, if not, then you may have to walk away, even if the initiative has several other merits. On the surface, the price tag for the product or service itself often seems clear. A multisite license for a reading program may cost $30,000 annually. A set of new history books might total $260,000. A Chromebook cart can be purchased for $7,500. However, there may be hidden costs in a new initiative, not to mention the ongoing support needed beyond the initial investment. Taking into account all the vital resources can reduce unnecessary obstacles.

Let's say the initiative is implementing an onboarding system for new employees. The online platform costs $8,000 for the setup and transfer of data from the district's information system, along with an annual $35,000 fee to use the program's features. It sounds like an inexpensive option that will transfer old-school practices into an easier-to-use digital format. But what about the staff time that will need to be redirected from other duties in the administration and information technology departments to learn and launch the solution? Also consider the required training to bring everyone up to speed on the program. What happens after the tech support sunsets at the end of the first year? This is a simple example that also can be applied to more complex or larger initiatives. Therefore, it's important to keep in mind the applicable costs as they specifically relate to the type of endeavor.

GUIDING QUESTIONS

- What funding sources are available for the initiative?
- Is the chosen funding source ongoing or temporary? General or restricted?
- What are the anticipated costs for the following?
  - Professional development
  - Materials
  - Technologies
  - Curriculum or licenses
  - Human resources
  - Ongoing support
  - Contingency funds for cost overruns or unforeseen circumstances

Some of the questions embedded in these six steps will not yield immediate answers but are there to spark awareness of the bigger picture and elements for future examination. The rationale for developing the initiative is the first hurdle to jump. After the rationale passes muster, then delving into the questions contained in values alignment, history or background, and forecasting future stages will shore up the primitive proposition. Finally, it's time to get down to the nuts and bolts of how stakeholders might react and secure resources for the initiative's long-term success.

CONCLUSION

This research and vetting stage may result in a significant metamorphosis from the original concept into something different. It can be tempting to think that the *first* idea is the *right* idea. But by pulling it apart and putting it back together again, one may find that the initial pursuit was seeking a cure for the wrong ailment. As we're still quite early in the process, it's crucial to preserve any useful nuggets unearthed in this first stage. These rich discussions should prompt the team leader back to the drawing board to flesh out the proposal he or she will pitch to the leadership team in the development stage that follows.

STAGE 1 ACTION PLAN: CHECKLIST AND REPRODUCIBLE

The following checklist and reproducible help you apply what you learned in this chapter and move forward to the next stage of the initiative implementation process.

- ☐ Carefully select your leadership team members.
- ☐ Embed the seven effective leadership practices in your team training.
- ☐ Complete the six steps in the research and vetting process using the "Initiative Vetting Notetaking Tool."

Initiative Vetting Notetaking Tool

Directions: This notetaking tool will help you make your way through the six steps in the stage 1 research and vetting process. The left-hand column lists the steps, and the right-hand column is a place to check off the elements as you hear them addressed in the initiative presentation. Even if the presentation covers each item listed, it does not account for the degree to which the leader or school has satisfied each criterion. That will be handled in the next stage.

Stage 1 Steps	Proposal Components
Step 1: Identify the rationale or reason for developing the initiative.	☐ Answers the *why* ☐ Enhances student learning ☐ Solves a known problem
Step 2: Develop awareness and alignment around the proposal.	☐ Aligns with district demographics ☐ Supports the district's vision and values ☐ Reflects community expectations
Step 3: Tap into history and background.	☐ Demonstrates understanding of the relationship to past initiatives ☐ Fits into existing district frameworks or strategic plans ☐ Considers past missteps
Step 4: Forecast the future.	☐ Impacts student learning ☐ Prepares students for the future ☐ Evolves or adapts to changing conditions
Step 5: Anticipate the impact on and reaction of stakeholders.	☐ Plans to engage those it impacts ☐ Includes strategies to develop support ☐ Includes strategies to address opposition

Step 6: Brainstorm estimated costs.	☐ Identifies potential funding sources
	 ☐ Considers costs for:
	   ☐ Professional development
	   ☐ Materials
	   ☐ Technologies
	   ☐ Curriculum or licenses
	   ☐ Human resources
	   ☐ Ongoing support
	   ☐ Contingencies (for example, cost overruns, unforeseen circumstances)

CHAPTER 2

Stage 2: Pitch the Proposal

If it seems as if it's taken an awfully long time to get to stage 2, that's not an illusion. A lot of heavy lifting has already taken place and important work carried out. Since the initiative hasn't already been abandoned, it means it has legs, and the leadership team leader is ready to commit it to paper.

Proposal development can be done in narrative style, slideshow presentation format, or a combination of the two. One way to think of the pitch is as storytelling. The first part of the plot lays down the basic foundation for the idea itself, followed by how the idea (or story) unfolds, and then the ways in which the idea resolves a central problem or conflict. The beginning should hook the audience, the middle should explain the problem that the idea will address, and the conclusion should wrap up the narrative with a recommendation. This chapter introduces you to a calibration tool called a *tuning protocol* for the leadership team to utilize during the team leader's first formal presentation on the topic, as well as a diagnostic notetaking form that will result in uncovering the gaps and opportunities ahead.

TUNING PROTOCOL

There is a wide variety of approaches for using protocols in professional settings to vet new initiatives. McDonald and colleagues (2013) write:

> The protocols have been adapted countless times in many settings for diverse purposes. They are popular too because each implicitly teaches one of three but rare important skills: the first, how to give and receive safe and honest feedback; the second, how to analyze complex problems carefully and without rushing to judgment; and the third, how to ground interpretations of complex texts. (p. 1)

There are a host of methods to choose from, all with the same goal of helping the leadership team get in tune with the rest of the school or district.

The primary objective of the tuning protocol is to obtain feedback from colleagues about the degree to which a proposal is ready. The tuning protocol in figure 2.1 delineates the roles, responsibilities, and participation guidelines for the participants in the exercise. Using this structured discussion tool, the leadership team leader delivers a presentation for colleagues who serve as critical friends. They are there to compassionately and honestly offer feedback to improve the leader's proposal. They are also there to support the team leader by looking for gaps, presenting alternatives, providing distinct lenses, and helping the leader craft the plan. Some of these individuals will serve in this sole capacity as initial thought partners and not end up participating on the forthcoming leadership team, while others will continue along the journey. I refer to this vetting body as the *consulting team*.

Tuning Protocol

When you tune a plan, you have two basic components: a set of goals and a set of activities sequenced in a way to help your group meet those goals. The objective is to get feedback from colleagues about the degree to which the activities seem likely to help the group achieve these goals. The plan is in tune when the goals and activities are in alignment. This is also critical for your new initiative to move into the implementation stage.

Presentation to Address These Issues (fifteen minutes)

- ☐ Description of initiative
- ☐ Why you are bringing forward the initiative
- ☐ How the initiative aligns with existing district frameworks, initiatives, and mission and vision
- ☐ The data driving this need
- ☐ The intended impact on teaching and learning
- ☐ How you will measure that impact
- ☐ The anticipated timeline from conception to full launch
- ☐ Resources needed (personnel, training, materials, technology, time)
- ☐ Stakeholder engagement
- ☐ Regular communications

Clarifying Questions (three minutes)

- ☐ Clarifying questions pertain to matters that can be answered factually or in a few short words. Save substantive issues for later.
- ☐ The protocol facilitator, not the team leader, is responsible for making sure that clarifying questions are really clarifying.

> **Individual Feedback (two minutes)**
> - ☐ Participants write down *warm* and *cool* feedback to share in the whole-group discussion.
> - ☐ They can phrase warm feedback as "I like . . ." or "I appreciate . . ." to show favorable reactions.
> - ☐ They can phrase cool feedback as "I wonder . . ." or "You may consider . . ." to prompt further thinking and discussion.
>
> **Group Feedback (fifteen minutes)**
> - ☐ Participants talk to each other about the presenter's plan (as if the presenter is not in the room), beginning with the ways the plan seems likely to meet the goals, continuing with possible disconnects and problems, and perhaps ending with one or two probing questions for further reflection by the presenter.
>
> **Presenter Reaction (five minutes)**
> - ☐ The team leader talks about what he or she has learned from the consulting team's feedback. This is *not* a time to defend oneself, but a time to explore further interesting ideas that came out of the feedback section. At any point, the presenter may open the conversation to the entire group (or not).
>
> **Next Steps and Debrief (five minutes)**
> - ☐ The consulting team discusses next steps for the initiative.
> - ☐ The facilitator leads an open discussion of this tuning experience.

Source: Adapted from McDonald & Allen, 2021.

Figure 2.1: Tuning protocol.

*Visit **go.SolutionTree.com/leadership** for a free reproducible version of this figure.*

Fashioning the proposal based on the conversations that took place in stage 1 and input provided on the "Initiative Vetting Notetaking Tool" (page 19), the leadership team leader designs his or her presentation to cover items outlined in the tuning protocol. The entire tuning protocol can be accomplished within an hour or more if needed. The team leader spends up to fifteen minutes delivering the presentation, while others listen without interruption. Then the consulting team has three minutes to ask clarifying questions. Clarifying questions tend to matters of fact that can usually be answered in a word or short explanation. A carefully chosen neutral facilitator from the consulting team is responsible for making sure that clarifying questions are really explanatory and that substantive issues are saved for later. Some examples of clarifying questions include the following.

- "What was the main research base you referred to?"
- "Did I understand you when you said . . . ?"
- "What criteria did you use to . . . ?"

- "Did I paraphrase what you meant correctly?"
- "Can you explain the chart, graph, or data again, so I make sure I understand?"
- "Did you take into account what additional resources might cost?"
- "Does the timeline include a place for feedback?"

The presenter answers each question to ensure that people understand the intentions, definitions, and details adequately before moving on.

It's then time to pause to allow for individual reactions. Each person writes down *warm* and *cool* feedback to share in the whole-group discussion. Cool should not be equated with negative, however, and is not meant to criticize the leadership team leader or the initiative.

The next fifteen minutes is designated for collective feedback when consulting team members talk to each other about the plan as if the team leader is not in the room. They begin with the ways that the plan seems likely to meet the goals, continue with possible disconnects and problems, and end with a couple of probing questions for further reflection on the part of the presenter. Probing questions might be framed as follows.

- "What do you think would happen if . . . ?"
- "What sort of impact do you think . . . ?"
- "How did you decide . . . ?"
- "How did you conclude . . . ?"
- "What is the connection between this initiative and . . . ?"
- "What is the most compelling evidence to gain support for this?"
- "What needs to change in order for us to accomplish this?"
- "If you were a (teacher, parent, student, board member, superintendent), how might you perceive this proposal differently?"

Following this fishbowl-style discussion, the presenter talks about what he or she has learned from the participants' feedback. This is not a time to defend oneself but an opportunity to explore further interesting ideas that came out of the feedback section. The final five minutes are to discuss next steps and debrief the process.

TWO REAL-WORLD SCENARIOS

The following two hypothetical new initiative proposals (Proposal Example A and Proposal Example B) illustrate how the tuning protocol works.

The leadership team leader in the first scenario is the director of secondary education in a medium-sized suburban district. Comparing her own district's science pathways to the surrounding districts on the heels of the NGSS adoption, and consulting with the high school principals, she asserts they should consider moving from a two-year to a three-year graduation requirement. Figure 2.2 contains key points from her presentation to directors of other groups or teams (for example, special education, student services, curriculum and instruction) and the assistant superintendent in the instructional services division.

Proposal Example A: Change the science graduation requirement from two years to three years for all students in the district.	
1. Description of initiative	• In 2013, the California State Board of Education adopted the Next Generation Science Standards (NGSS). • The high school NGSS have added content areas and are greater in number than previous standards. • NGSS requires concepts be taught through the science and engineering practices and, therefore, require a greater depth of instruction. • More than half of our students already take three years of science. • Therefore, it makes sense to shift to a three-year high school science graduation requirement.

2. Why it's being brought forward	• The NGSS are for all students, not just those planning careers in science and technology.
	• All students, no matter what their future education and career path, must have a solid K–12 science education to be prepared for college, careers, and citizenship.
	• When provided with equitable learning opportunities, students from diverse backgrounds can engage in scientific practices and construct meaning for success in the science classroom.
	• Our graduation requirement in science is not enough time to teach all the high school NGSS.
	    ♦ Life science: twenty-four standards
	    ♦ Physical science: twenty-four standards
	    ♦ Earth and space science: nineteen standards
	    ♦ Engineering, technology, and application to science: four standards

Figure 2.2: Proposal example A.

continued ▶

	Proposal Example A: Change the science graduation requirement from two years to three years for all students in the district.
	• Changing the high school science graduation requirement to three years will address this problem. • This new initiative will give all students the opportunity to develop the habits of mind and critical thinking required by the NGSS. • Upcoming nationwide assessments will test all NGSS high school standards.
3. How it aligns with existing district frameworks, initiatives, and mission and vision	• Commitment to equity: Three years of science will create more equitable conditions for students. • 21st century learning environment: It supports a guaranteed and viable curriculum across the district. • Graduate profile: It prepares all students for post-secondary college and provides career readiness for STEM (science, technology, engineering, and mathematics) opportunities. • Alignment: The California Science Framework contains only a three-year course model or a four-year course model.

4. The data driving this need	• In our district, 56 percent of students take three or more years of science. Therefore, 44 percent of students are less competitive for admission to four-year colleges and have less opportunity to develop the critical thinking skills required in the NGSS.
	• According to a 2018 study conducted by the ACT:
	  ♦ 45% of 2018 graduates—approximately 853,000 students—were interested in STEM majors or occupations, down from 48% in 2017.
	  ♦ The average national STEM score was 20.9 in 2018, down from 21.1 in 2017.
	  ♦ 20% of 2018 graduates met the ACT STEM Readiness Benchmark, down from 21% last year but steady with the three previous years.
	  ♦ Underserved students lag far behind their peers in the area of STEM. Consistent with last year, only 2% of students meeting all three underserved criteria achieved the STEM benchmark (p. 2).

5. The intended impact on teaching and learning	• Teachers will have more time to effectively address and teach all the NGSS standards. • More, if not all, students will have the foundation to pursue STEM college programs and careers. • All students will have three years of science to develop the habits of mind and critical thinking skills for success in college and global citizenship.

6. How we will measure the impact	- Performance on California State Science Assessment
- Consistent graduation rates
- Increased acceptance rate to four-year colleges and universities
- Increased enrollment in STEM-related fields of study
7. The anticipated timeline from conception to full launch	- Current year: Develop course descriptions and get them board and state approved.
- Year 1: Offer NGSS freshman class.
- Year 2: Offer NGSS sophomore class.
- Year 3: Offer NGSS junior class.
- Year 4: First-year, NGSS-aligned freshman course is required for all incoming ninth graders.
8. Resources needed	- Professional development or summer training plus release days for two years: $53,000
- Addition of lab classrooms or repurposing of non-lab classrooms: $869,000
- NGSS textbook adoption: $4.7 million
- Consumable lab materials per year times four high schools: $36,000
- Additional staffing of eight full-time-equivalent employees (FTEs): $750,000
9. Stakeholder engagement	- Site visits
- Parent and community forums
- Student survey
- Principals' meetings
10. Communications planning	- Curriculum and instruction newsletter
- Superintendent's update
- Board meeting informational presentations
- Video and post classroom model lessons
- Create a FAQs (frequently asked questions) section for the district website
- Share links to the state department of education

PROPOSAL EXAMPLE A

Change the Science Graduation Requirement From Two Years to Three Years for All Students in the District

After the leader delivers her fifteen-minute presentation, the consulting team spends three minutes asking the following clarifying questions.

- "Do we currently have enough teachers in our district with the appropriate credentials to teach the additional sections?"
- "Did you consult with the facilities department on the costs to bring all the existing science labs up to code?"
- "Does this mean fewer students are able to take elective courses in their junior year? Will electives teachers lose their jobs?"
- "Does year one on the timeline include a pilot year or a full start next fall?"
- "Do the courses have approved materials available from the state department of education?"

The facilitator answers each question, and then participants spend a few minutes writing down their *warm* and *cool* feedback. They go around the room, one by one, sharing their thoughts.

- "I like that we are going to be in better alignment with the neighboring districts."
- "I appreciate that you want to raise the bar for all students."
- "I agree that we need to communicate really clearly with all stakeholder groups."
- "I wonder if the state will really have the framework and curriculum ready by the time we want to put this in place."
- "I wonder if this will result in an increase of high school dropouts if the third year of science is too challenging."
- "You should check in with the district's human resources department to find out what it will take to recruit and hire eight full-time-equivalent employees (FTE) when there is already a science teacher shortage in our state."
- "We may want to look instead at all our high school graduation requirements before considering science in a silo."

Building on the individual feedback they heard, consulting team members then spend fifteen minutes discussing the presenter's plan. While there is general philosophical agreement that more science is a good thing for students, there are many concerns about the implications of making a large-scale change in graduation requirements.

The director of special education worries about creating more barriers for students with disabilities and wants to know what additional supports will be provided for them.

The director of federal and state programs chimes in saying that she has the same concerns for the district's 32 percent English learners, since the academic vocabulary in science can be very difficult to comprehend.

The assistant superintendent asks the director of curriculum and instruction, "Can we really trust that the state will have materials ready for us by next fall? It seems as if they usually deliver a year or two behind schedule." He shrugs and replies, "I wouldn't count on it, but my department can assist with curriculum development if needed." "I'm not sure that's a great strategy if we have to create everything from scratch," she frowns.

The director of elementary education says, "I'm a little worried about teacher readiness and buy-in. I know we can technically assign teachers to any class they are credentialed in, but is that what's best for students if a person doesn't have the skill or will to teach the NGSS as intended? I think we need more professional development in this area."

The director of student services suggests that they should find out how the other local districts made the shift and see what lessons they can apply to this initiative.

The conversation concludes with the assistant superintendent polling each consulting team member to see, on a scale of 1 to 5, how ready they are to back this proposal. One finger indicates serious reservations about the plan, and five fingers mean full support. Most directors hold up three fingers, suggesting a middle level of support, so she turns it back over to the team leader.

The director of secondary education is furiously writing notes throughout the discussion. She thanks her colleagues for the great questions they posed and acknowledges some of their concerns. "I'm glad you brought up the teacher training and credentialing issue. If we do go to a three-year model, it will mean hiring plus reassigning existing teachers to other courses. We probably need a longer timeframe than I'd planned for." She continues, "I don't want us to wait too long, however, because our students will be tested on all the NGSS, and we are doing them a disservice by not providing the whole span of curriculum." After responding to some of her colleagues' other comments, she turns to the team for a verdict.

The assistant superintendent takes another poll, and response is still lukewarm. She concludes, "I think there are enough gaps that we need to have answers to before committing to this proposal. Bring us back hard data on staffing, the impact on the master schedule at each of the four schools, the timeline for materials adoption, and then meet with the science curriculum council to get their suggestions as well."

Although the proposal did not result in an immediate *yes*, team members collectively agree that it's worth examining further. The team leader heads back to the drawing board and plans to make another presentation in two months' time.

They finish up the protocol by debriefing the process, and everyone agrees they learned something from each other's perspectives that they wouldn't have initially seen. Those engaged in the discussion benefited from witnessing their colleague go through the process and will make sure their own proposals cover all necessary bases when it's their turn.

While the first example, Proposal Example A, illustrates an instructional initiative, the second example is operational in nature. In Proposal Example B, a rural district seeks to tighten its fiscal belt and also become more environmentally responsive. All five elementary schools in the district and the central office will be expected to move to digital platforms in lieu of printing out hard copies of lesson plans, communications, report cards, and other paper-heavy endeavors. This venture will require a shift in culture, mentality, and practice.

Figure 2.3 (page 30) contains key points from the district's chief business official's (CBO) role in the hot seat as the leadership team leader in the following scenario.

Proposal Example B: Embrace a more environmentally conscious and fiscally responsible plan to reduce paper usage by 50 percent.	
1. Description of initiative	- The business services division, in partnership with human resources and instructional services, propose reducing paper use in the district by 50 percent. - Remove personal printers from offices and classrooms and replace them with copiers and printers in centralized areas. - Send all newsletters and communications via email and post them on the district website. - Allot a finite paper allowance to employees for the year.
2. Why it's being brought forward	- This is the 21st century, and we have many electronic means other than paper with which to communicate. - The future climate and environment rely on us to change our practices for long-term sustainability. - There is too much waste, and we need to do our part in reducing it and be better role models for our students. - People are already familiar with email, text, and the internet, and almost everyone has access to information via smartphones or other devices.
3. How it aligns with existing district frameworks, initiatives, and mission and vision	- Our mission is to create a better world for the future, and this aligns perfectly. - We are committed to fiscal solvency. Cutting paper consumption by 50 percent will allow us to use that money for site-based digital devices for staff and student use.
4. The data driving this need	- We currently spend over $500,000 on paper and printer ink each year. Reducing costs by 50 percent will allow us to use those funds for other educational purposes. - Many U.S. companies have already gone paperless. We are behind the curve. - According to a recent survey, over 93 percent of our families have access to a 3G network or the internet, and they already use their devices for getting information.
5. The intended impact on teaching and learning	- The intention is to free up funding that's being wasted on printing and paper and use it to modernize our classrooms. - Students today are digital natives and can easily navigate technologies. They also need to use devices in future jobs, so this will help meet that goal. - Teachers have already shifted to using Google Classroom and the suite of apps and have less need to print out classwork or homework for students.

6. How we will measure the impact	- Technology infrastructure upgrades throughout the district equals faster internet - Investment in new devices for teaching and learning - Student completion of homework and classwork as reported through the online report card
7. The anticipated timeline from conception to full launch	Year one: - August–September: District office tries it out - October: Formally introduce initiative - January: Kick-off campaign - May: Gather feedback from employees, parents, and students - June: Account for cost savings from January–June Year two: - July: Set new reduction goal for the upcoming school year
8. Resources needed	- Information kiosk in every school office and district office for parents without access to technology: $35,000 - High-speed internet connection at all sites: included in bond funding - Training for staff to use technology more effectively: $9,500 - Information technology staff overtime for the first six months of support: $14,000 - Licenses for communication tools to reach parents and the community: $24,000
9. Stakeholder engagement	- District office staff will lead by example by going fully digital in August. - All communications will be sent via online platforms, and the district will cease all paper communications to staff and families. - The superintendent will poll the community to see how the shift is being received in October. - Feedback will be used to make adjustments to the initiative. - The community will be invited to participate in the "Go Green" paper reduction campaign. - A contest will be held at all sites from January–June to see who can save the most paper. - Progress will be celebrated at an end-of-year community function, and new goals will be set for the next year.

Figure 2.3: Proposal example B.

continued ▶

Proposal Example B: Embrace a more environmentally conscious and fiscally responsible plan to reduce paper usage by 50 percent.	
10. Communications planning	• Post district and site newsletters online. • Use social media to promote environmental tips. • Present the initiative at a board meeting. • Create a "trees saved" thermometer for each school. • Survey stakeholders.

PROPOSAL EXAMPLE B

Embrace a More Environmentally Conscious and Fiscally Responsible Plan to Reduce Paper Usage by 50 Percent

When the CBO finishes an enthusiastic presentation of his innovative proposal to the district management team, he activates the first steps of the tuning protocol. A few clarifying questions lead into the heart of the discussion. Warm feedback includes excitement about the efforts to redirect funding from paper products to digital tools, the positive impact on the environment, and the recognition that we don't really need paper in the same way we used to. Some of the cooler responses relate to the huge shift required for teachers to change the way they deliver instruction, the potential backlash from office staff who can't keep their own printers, and concern about equity for students and families without as much technology at home.

When consulting team members flesh out these topics further, they suggest modifying the plans by using a phased-in approach. Originally, full implementation was supposed to begin in January. Upon further dialogue, they agree to roll back the launch to begin only with non-instructional staff. Instead of expecting teachers to significantly change their instruction, assessment, and reporting practices mid-year, the initiative will not be fully scaled until August of the following year. The organizer accepts these suggestions and tweaks the details of the plan to incorporate the staggered implementation. When they debrief the process, the CBO's enthusiasm is still intact but tempered to approach the implementation more deliberately.

After a tuning protocol is complete, the leadership team leader may want to pursue additional conversations with individual team members to tackle some of the cool feedback he or she heard. The goal is to strengthen the underdeveloped parts of the proposal so there are fewer weak links to derail it. While the person spearheading the initiative very likely thinks it should be elevated to one of the most important focuses in the district, he or she must consider environmental readiness and the context for its inclusion. Therefore, carefully reflecting on how this initiative fits in the bigger picture sets the stage for the prioritization part of the protocol.

CONCLUSION

This chapter's focus on teamwork and the early vetting process is the first foray into the new initiatives process. The leadership team leader, which will change depending on each initiative's scope, convenes a consulting team to run through a first pass of ideas. It's like writing a first draft, trying out a new recipe, or hiking an unfamiliar trail. The consulting team provides high-level feedback, asks clarifying questions, and prompts the leadership team leader to expand on his or her own thinking or design. If there is enough momentum or enthusiasm to continue on to stage 3, this initial consulting team dissolves and is reconstituted into a more formal leadership team that will help the leadership team leader execute the rest of the process.

STAGE 2 ACTION PLAN: CHECKLIST AND REPRODUCIBLE

The following checklist and reproducibles help you apply what you learned in this chapter and move forward to the next stage of the initiative implementation process.

- ☐ Develop the tuning protocol (see figure 2.1, page 22).
- ☐ Complete the "Protocol-Planning Template" reproducible (page 34).
- ☐ Follow up on the suggestions offered at the end of the "Protocol-Planning Template."

Protocol-Planning Template

Directions: Take notes on this template during the team leader's tuning protocol presentation to help you identify strengths and gaps in the second stage of the new initiative implementation process.

Task	Notes	Time
Presentation 1. Description of initiative 2. Why it's being brought forward 3. How it aligns with existing district frameworks, initiatives, and mission and vision 4. The data driving this need 5. The intended impact on teaching and learning 6. How we will measure the impact 7. The anticipated timeline from conception to full launch 8. Resources needed 9. Stakeholder engagement 10. Regular communications		Twelve to fifteen minutes
Clarifying Questions		Three minutes
Individual Feedback		Two minutes

page 1 of 2

Leading the Launch © 2022 Solution Tree Press • SolutionTree.com
Visit **go.SolutionTree.com/leadership** to download this page.

Group Feedback		Fifteen minutes
Presenter Reaction		Five minutes
Next Steps and Debrief		Five minutes

Suggestions

Further define the need or the *why*:

Expand or reduce focus area to:

Lay more groundwork by:

Gather more data from:

Do more research on:

Secure financial resources:

Get stakeholder buy-in from:

Flesh out details regarding:

Adjust the timing or schedule:

Talk to or consult with:

Other:

CHAPTER 3

Stage 3: Determine Priorities

Not all initiatives are created equal, and thus, must not be considered in a vacuum. Prioritizing is a mental exercise that effective leaders naturally do every day. Administrators are masterminds at multitasking. At times, however, the sheer volume of inquiries, emails, phone calls, emergencies, and interactions can make it all too easy to lose track of the forest for the trees. There is only so much mental space to juggle the demands of the job, much less execute a strategic plan.

In this stage, it's time to take a good hard look at all of the competing initiatives collectively on paper. By outlining the commitments that the school or district has already made and charting their progress in relationship to each other, leaders can gain a different and wider-spread outlook.

This chapter tackles the ways in which you can whittle down and organize the core initiatives analytically and pragmatically in your school or district. The tools and insights provided can help you clear the forest so you can see the trees before planting any new ones that will thrive.

INITIATIVE OVERLOAD

A school district is an active entity with multifaceted needs and often competing interests. Yet we simply can't do everything. A case in point is the Common Core State Standards (CCSS) in English language arts (ELA) and mathematics. The writers of the standards themselves could not agree on how to reduce the number of items to fit within a thirteen-year, K–12 grade span. A widespread mythology surrounding the CCSS is that to truly teach to mastery, the ELA standards would take approximately twenty-three years. This has resulted in most districts picking and choosing priority standards, which are the must-teach rather than the nice-to-teach objectives.

School district initiatives can face the same problem if the scope of a new initiative is not well managed and balanced with other ongoing endeavors.

Figure 3.1 illustrates how a district might have simultaneous initiatives related to programs, projects, or endeavors that may be competing for resources and attention. The goal in the prioritizing stage is not necessarily to eliminate implementations, but to coordinate and schedule them in a methodical manner by funneling them through this stage in the process.

Figure 3.1: Managing multiple implementations.

Tony Frontier and James Rickabaugh (2014) identify five "levers" for prioritizing school improvement efforts to help avoid misalignment of effort and resources. They define a *lever* as:

> A means or device used to accomplish something that otherwise might not have been possible. In physical terms, a lever is useful because it dramatically increases the amount of weight that can be lifted on one end of the lever given a limited amount of force applied to the other end. (p. 10)

This concept, when applied to school settings, explains how you can accomplish more with less power or energy when you recognize the key elements to weigh on the balance beam.

Frontier and Rickabaugh (2014) further identify the five areas that leaders can leverage to increase the impact of initiatives:

> The five levers are *structure, sample, standards, strategy,* and *self. Structure* refers to logistical components such as schedules, bells, and class size. *Sample* involves grouping of students in classrooms, programs, or learning opportunities at any given time. *Standards* include practices associated with expectations for student learning. *Strategy* refers to instructional strategies used to manage classrooms and engage students in meaningful learning experiences. *Self* includes the set of beliefs that teachers and students have about their capacity to be effective. (p. 19)

CRITERIA FOR PREVENTING INITIATIVE OVERLOAD

Building on this concept of leverage, I created a rubric (see figure 3.2) with weighted criteria to help leaders determine placement in context of the overall rollout of other initiatives and prevent system overload at the district level. A reproducible version of this figure is included at the end of this chapter (page 52).

Criteria or Weight	Guiding Questions	Rating Scale
Criteria 1: Strategic Alignment Weight = 1	To what extent is the project aligned with the department or site's vision, mission, and goals? To what extent is the project aligned with existing frameworks or strategic plans?	1 = Does not align 2 = Some alignment 3 = Full alignment
Criteria 2: Connection to Other Initiatives Weight = 2	To what degree does the project intersect with or support other district initiatives? To what degree will the project lay a foundation to support future initiatives?	1 = None; stands alone 2 = Intersects; supports some 3 = Intersects; supports all
Criteria 3: Impact on Learning Weight = 3	*Consider what the data says about why this initiative is needed.* To what extent will the project positively impact student learning? How widespread will the project's impact be across the district?	1 = Low impact 2 = Medium impact 3 = High impact

Figure 3.2: Initiative prioritization rubric.

continued ▶

Criteria or Weight	Guiding Questions	Rating Scale
Criteria 4: Equity *Weight = 2*	To what extent will the project increase equity for students? To what extent does it address the specific, data-driven needs of diverse student groups?	1 = No increase 2 = Some increase 3 = Significant increase
Criteria 5: Support From Key Stakeholders *Weight = 2*	What is the level of support from other district office departments (human resources, business, superintendent) or the school board? What is the level of support from employee associations? What is the level of support from parents, students, the community at large, and the business community?	1 = Unknown or weak level of support 2 = Support from some 3 = Complete support
Criteria 6: Timing or Readiness *Weight = 2*	*Consider the urgency of the problem being solved.* To what degree is the district ready for this initiative? To what degree is this the right time for this initiative?	1 = Not ready; too early to tell 2 = Adequately prepared; good timing 3 = Totally prepared; perfect timing
Criteria 7: Required Service *Weight = 2*	Is the project required to meet legal, compliance, or regulatory mandates? Does this project fulfill a moral or ethical obligation? Is the project responsive to concerns being brought up by staff, students, or parents?	1 = Not required or mandated 2 = Not required but has ethical value 3 = Required or mandated by law
Criteria 8: Costs and Resources *Weight = 2*	What is the potential cost-benefit of the project? What are the other resources, other than money, needed to sustain the effort?	1 = High potential for unknown or unexpected costs 2 = Some costs are known and planned for 3 = All costs, direct and indirect, are known, planned for, and budgeted

STRATEGIC ALIGNMENT

As mentioned earlier, evaluating how a new initiative aligns to other district enterprises helps to find the right place for it in the scheme of things. Ideally, it should have a direct correlation to the department or site's vision, mission, and goals. Existing frameworks or strategic plans also need to be cross-checked to ensure that the effort is not duplicating what's already in play nor completely out in left field. The target is finding that sweet spot of filling a need already identified in the values of the school or district while building on the other work.

Many school districts have developed roadmaps outlining the pathways for student outcomes. A trending strategic planning model is called a graduation profile or portrait of a graduate. These profiles (or portraits) list the desired attributes students will develop and attain by the time they graduate. Other types of strategic, accountability, or accreditation plans can also serve as guides. Depending on state or local ordinances, almost every district is required to fill out and submit annual blueprints, such as the Local Control and Accountability Plan (LCAP) in California; maintain accreditation through an outside entity such as the Western Association of Schools and Colleges (WASC); or meet national standards as outlined in the Every Student Succeeds Act (ESSA). Since many of these plans overlap, the objective is to leverage and strengthen preexisting goals as well as furnish a unifying framework to hold the work of the district.

Figure 3.3 is a snapshot of how three such plans can be synchronized on several fronts. This tool will help leaders from getting overwhelmed by the distractions that they face on a daily basis. While we must attend to the fires burning around us, as that is a significant part of the job, we should always look to the roadmap on the horizon beyond the smoke. So before a new initiative hits the ground, it needs to find its place within the master plans and have enough alignment to justify moving forward.

1. **U.S. Department of Education Title I Plan:** In order to better educate historically marginalized and underserved student groups, all schools and districts receiving the Title I, Part A federal funding must develop a plan outlining supports and services to meet the needs and improve academic outcomes for their students. (U.S. Department of Education, Title I Part A)

2. **Local Accountability Plans:** Many states, counties, and provinces are required by their governments to develop a multi-year plan that describes the goals, actions, services, and expenditures to support positive student outcomes that address local priorities.

3. **District Portrait of a Graduate:** Some school districts are creating a local strategic plan to unite under a common vision and mission by developing a roadmap of a well-rounded graduate with the qualities, experiences, character, skills, and knowledge he or she should attain along the way.

Figure 3.3: Sample district plans crosswalk.

continued ▶

Key Components	Title I	Local Plan	Portrait of a Graduate
Capacity Building and Leadership Development	•	•	
Curriculum and Instruction: Design and Delivery		•	•
Alignment of Instructional Materials and Methodologies	•	•	•
Professional Development	•	•	
Student Learning and Feedback Systems	•	•	•
Technology Support for Instruction, Data, and Assessment		•	
Parent Involvement	•	•	
Student Engagement	•	•	•
School Climate and Culture	•	•	
Student Transitions to Higher Education and Careers		•	•
Social-Emotional Learning			•

*Visit **go.SolutionTree.com/leadership** for a free reproducible version of this figure.*

CONNECTION TO OTHER INITIATIVES

After determining the initiative's alignment within the district's overall mission, vision, or preexisting strategic plan, we need to look at to what degree the project intersects with or supports other district or school initiatives. A district that has passed a large facilities bond, for example, must map out the relationships between the various maintenance and upgrades across the city's schools. In order to be fiscally prudent with taxpayer dollars, the leadership team should figure out ways to consolidate and expedite overlapping like projects. Replacing all the outdated fluorescent lighting in every parking lot may dovetail nicely with simultaneously installing solar panels. Too often, however, related projects are still handled in a vacuum and otherwise avoidable conflicts can arise as well as expensive mistakes.

It's a little bit like fitting together pieces of a jigsaw puzzle to reveal the whole picture. Spending time on the front end and linking together different initiatives will not only streamline but also supply a solid base for the new proposal. Likewise, we should look beyond this new initiative, which will at some point no longer be new, and imagine how it could lay a foundation for upcoming work. The last thing we want is for one initiative to undermine the work of another—now or in the future. Displaying all the initiatives on a table, literally, in a physical exercise may help unveil hidden connections and potential friction.

When we include people "from all sides of the house" (for example, business, instruction, and human resources), it can better expose gaps and opportunities. Human resources may foresee violations of a collective bargaining agreement or potential labor dispute. Instructional services may caution about the number of adoptions already increasing the workload of the site principals this year, and business services may caution that the initiative's funding source will be going away in two years and it just isn't in the budget beyond that point. These are the checks and balances needed when examining any project. Alternatively, the three departments collaborating together may identify places to save costs, time, and other resources by strategically clustering a series of initiatives together.

IMPACT ON LEARNING

The graduate profile or a local accountability plan can also be referenced to correlate how the new initiative is intended to impact student learning. Depending on community consensus, the attributes selected as focus areas for the district will range from academic to social-emotional to behavioral to extracurricular outcomes. While affording all kinds of student learning opportunities is imperative, the leadership team should rank these opportunities by importance.

An excellent model for levying value on the different initiatives is a school or district that functions as a professional learning community (PLC). The main thrust behind a PLC is a focus on learning, rather than teaching, and that focused teacher collaboration will positively impact student achievement. It consists of identifying what to teach, analyzing how well students are acquiring the new learning, and developing ways to support learners on each end of the spectrum—those who are or are not proficient. Applying the four critical questions of a PLC can solidify the purpose behind an instructional initiative by connecting it to one or more of the following questions (DuFour et al., 2016).

- What is it we want our students to know and be able to do? (content standards and skills)
- How will we know if each student has learned it? (formative assessment)
- How will we respond when some students do not learn it? (intervention)
- How will we extend the learning for students who have demonstrated proficiency? (extension)

Many curriculum-focused initiatives naturally huddle under one particular umbrella; the connections to other existing programs are many. Early learners' literacy instruction, for instance, includes a multitude of factors, such as the building blocks of phonemic awareness, decoding, fluency, vocabulary, text comprehension, written expression, and spelling and handwriting. Let's say the proposal is geared toward improving academic language skills for English learners. Multiple measures should be employed to home in on the type of materials or program that directly impact student reclassification rates, from *English learner* to *fluent-English proficient*, acquiring English language fluency is a nuanced undertaking. It's not just learning new vocabulary or grammatical syntax; it's also about a student's language of origin, immigration conditions, socioeconomic status, family engagement, and many other intangible factors. Language is personal, political, and socially constructed. Therefore, the more background knowledge we have, the better. Understanding how the program bolsters or replaces what's in existence is essential, and having the clearest idea of the end goal is paramount.

Impact on learning stems from PLC critical question 2: "How will we know if each student has learned it?" (DuFour et al., 2016, p. 59). So having the right assessment tools is key. It's not uncommon over time for schools or districts to select programs piecemeal to supersede what's already there. However, not every teacher or site administrator will readily let go of the familiar ways of doing things, even if their impact on learning is undetermined or negligible. Therefore, it's critical to lead with the data justifying the continuance, supplementing, or sunsetting of a legacy practice to make room for the new initiative.

EQUITY

Increasing equity for diverse student populations must be a serious determinant in the appraisal of any new initiative. If we don't have a sharp eye on equity, we may select a program, product, or service that actually widens achievement gaps between different groups instead of closing them. It's not enough to do no harm; those developing new initiatives must intentionally seek out or develop initiatives that meet the specific needs of particular learners.

Again, digging beneath the surface is indispensable to identify the true barriers to learning. When students come to school hungry or traumatized, no miraculous mathematics program in the world will restore them. A homeless high school student worried about not having clean clothes, much less ones that are in fashion, may not have her full attention on the college and career readiness curriculum. An undocumented eighth grader from El Salvador who works the night shift in his parents' bodega and keeps falling asleep in his first period English class might be missing out on key instruction that will help him acquire his second language.

All these scenarios are common in the United States, and some of the challenges facing students can seem insurmountable. A longitudinal study conducted by the National Center for Education Statistics (NCES) in 2018 (de Brey et al., 2019) reveals that we still have a lot of work to do to close the performance gaps among student groups in many areas of education, including access to resources, identification and placement, and academic achievement. Three years after the study's publication, updated statistics show little change.

> In 2019, the percentage of children under the age of 18 in families living in poverty was higher for Black children than Hispanic children (31 and 23 percent, respectively), and the percentages for both of these groups were higher than for White and Asian children (10 percent each). (de Brey et al., 2019, p. iv)

> The percentage of public school students in the United States who were English language learners (ELLs) was higher in fall 2018 (10.2 percent, or 5.0 million students) than in fall 2010 (9.2 percent, or 4.5 million students). In fall 2018, the percentage of public school students who were ELLs ranged from 0.8 percent in West Virginia to 19.4 percent in California. (NCES, 2021a)

> In school year 2019–20, the percentage of students served under IDEA was highest for American Indian/Alaska Native students (18 percent), followed by Black students (17 percent), and students of two or more races (15 percent), which were all at least one percentage point higher than the percentage of public school students served under IDEA overall (14 percent). The percentage was lowest for Pacific Islander students (11 percent) and Asian students (7 percent). (NCES, 2021b)

> At grade 4, the White-Black achievement gap in mathematics achievement scores narrowed from 32 points in 1990 to 25 points in 2017; the White-Hispanic gap in 2017 (19 points) was not measurably different from the gap in 1990. At grade 8, there was no measurable difference in the White-Black achievement gap in 2017 (32 points) and 1990. Similarly, the White-Hispanic achievement gap at grade 8 in 2017 (24 points) was not measurably different from the gap in 1990. (de Brey et al., 2019, p. iv)

> At grade 4, the White-Black gap in reading achievement scores narrowed from 32 points in 1992 to 26 points in 2017; the White-Hispanic gap in 2017 (23 points) was not measurably different from the gap in 1992. At grade 8, the White Hispanic gap narrowed from 26 points in 1992 to 19 points in 2017; the White-Black gap in 2017 (25 points) was not measurably different from the gap in 1992. (de Brey et al., 2019, p. iv)

All these statistics show why education is truly the most critical system in the United States, specifically, to elevate, provide hope, and create better conditions for the future.

Many students face external elements over which we have little control, but there are plenty that the educational system inadvertently fosters. What about using recess restriction to punish children with attention deficit hyperactivity disorder who are not on-task in class? What about the tardy policy penalizing the family that has no reliable transportation? What about the hetero-centric curriculum that discounts the contributions of or neglects to mention the sexuality of LGBTQ historical role models? Think about the immigrant child from India who, even though a native speaker of English, is ridiculed about her accent every time she raises her hand to participate, and the teacher fails to intervene. The list of microaggressions lining the woodwork of public education not only are hiding in plain sight but also often upheld and promoted.

This is not about making excuses or placing blame, but about increasing awareness—and doing better by our students. Ideally, educators should operate from the assumption that all students want to learn, want to feel good about themselves, and want us to be proud of them. This is evident in every kindergarten classroom—eager, excited, enthusiastic learners in every way, shape, and form. By the time they get older, however, the walls go higher and it is our job to either provide the ladder to help scale them or knock them down. Whether it's addressing hidden or overt bias, both manufactured within our institution and persisting in the outside world, it is essential that we look through the lens of equity in regard to prioritizing.

SUPPORT FROM KEY STAKEHOLDERS

Garnering support from stakeholders takes time and effort. It's beneficial if others already have a certain level of confidence in the leadership behind the initiative. If the person presenting the initiative has proven to deliver on past projects, communicates well, and is trusted by the community, the new idea may have a softer landing. Unfortunately, most things "coming down from the district" have earned the connotation as *out of touch*, *top down*, or some other "us versus them" construct. New ideas can easily be tainted by this perspective.

The power of support should not be underestimated. With the right people in our corner, an initiative can soar. With the same right people voicing dissent or detraction, it's as good as over. A coalition-building approach will help shore up the plans so when things inevitably hit a bump, there are enough proponents on board to keep the fence-sitters staying the course.

Research on engagement shows that attending to the following areas will result in improved decision making: casting a wide net to poll the school community, developing a shared vision among stakeholders and K–12 school leaders, including student voices to influence outcomes, and using multi-pronged communications with a diverse audience (Tran, Smith, & Buckman, 2020).

There are many stakeholders involved in public education—a variety of district office departments, the school board, employee associations, parents, students, the community at large, and local businesses. All too frequently, we miss out on testing the proof of concept widely enough. Perception is reality, so our primary job at the start is to craft perception by leveraging buy-in. I cannot emphasize enough that without key stakeholder support, there is little chance for initiative survival.

Decisions that affect classroom teachers must involve their input at the forefront. That's a given. We also need to think of the people outside the immediate domain that can make or break an initiative. A team can expend a huge amount of effort on a proposal only to have it land on the superintendent's desk and get a veto because she had a negative past experience with the vendor. Or the superintendent may favor the concept only to have it run afoul of a salary negotiations process gone sour, such that the teachers' union refuses to implement the plan if they believe it is coming from her office. Thus, it may favor the leader behind the initiative to gather momentum directly at the site level instead of presenting it as a district initiative. Strategy is everything when it comes to building support.

TIMING AND READINESS

Timing may be the next most critical factor in play, and it often goes hand in hand with stakeholder engagement. A common refrain heard throughout any one of nine-ish months of a school year is: "It's a bad time of year for x, y, or z." Any educator can recall hearing the following phrases: "People are *tired*." "The *holidays* are coming up." "That's *finals* week." "We're preparing for *state testing*." "*Report cards* are due." "We don't have time for *training*." "It's *winter/spring/almost summer*." We repeat these maxims as if they are factual and immovable. The bottom line is that *the* perfect time rarely exists, and we can wait forever to implement our plans if looking for the ideal moment.

That said, we should not discount the gravity of timing. The simple truth is that it's harder to start something new once the school year is underway. Professional development has been delivered, lessons preplanned, routines established, and habits formed. But that sparks the dilemma that a system cannot introduce everything all at once in August. While instructional initiatives are best infused in the system prior to the start of the school year, other functional changes, such as adopting a new facilities request system or moving from one email platform to another, can be a little more fluid.

When assessing where to start, one should consider the urgency of the endeavor. If the problem that needs to be solved is immediate, such as a compliance issue that will put the district at risk of a lawsuit if not resolved, that will drive the timeline.

Sometimes a district will have to put other initiatives waiting in line on hold when threatened with legal action or sanctions. Thankfully, those cases are not frequent.

For a voluntary initiative, one should weigh the degree to which the community is ready for the advancement and whether it's the right time. When comparing the initiative with others in the line, timing is a major part of the prioritizing process. Paired with the commensurate level of support, sometimes there is no time like the present. And sometimes, it's preferable to bide your time and wait.

REQUIRED SERVICE

As referenced previously, prioritizing may not always be a matter of choice but a mandate. State or federal legislation passes. Lawsuits are settled. Compliance requirements change. These cases are generally infused with moral or ethical obligations, but the people implementing them often have other feelings. If at all possible, packaging these statutes within other district values and goals can help move employees from compliance to commitment.

For example, let's say a district enters into a voluntary agreement with the state's Office of Civil Rights to mediate complaints that the local Muslim population has been experiencing discrimination and disenfranchisement. The agreement spells out the terms with which the district needs to comply to fulfill the settlement agreement. While addressing the specifics related to the identified protected class, the district's leadership team realizes that encompassing other religious and ethnic groups in the community would be beneficial. It's no secret that other religious minorities have also struggled in their schools. So they decide to go above and beyond the confines of the agreement and extend the remedies to their Sikh and Jewish populations as well. By expanding the scope, the district is organizing their efforts not only due to external requirements but also because it benefits everyone.

When the initiative is voluntary, commitment can be harder to come by, unless fueled by grassroots efforts. Though there is no legal compulsion, there may be moral, economic, or value-based incentives. A community struggling to fill high-tech jobs in the area can underscore the need for more STEM programs that prepare students for careers in these industries. An influx of social media harassment between middle schoolers can prompt an outcry for anti-bullying curriculum and training for teachers. These are not required, per se, but rather responsive to the concerns of the stakeholders.

Sometimes the leader may foster a greater sense of urgency for an initiative not otherwise required to forward the mission and vision of the district. Staying competitive with neighboring school systems, increasing college acceptance rates, or fulfilling community expectations all can be compelling reasons to push forth a new way of doing things. Whether required by law or responsive to needs, an initiative must have some reason compelling its momentum.

COSTS AND RESOURCES

Finally, we need to evaluate the resources to implement and sustain the initiative, including time, money, professional development, materials, technology, curriculum, human resources, facilities, and ongoing support. Conducting a cost-benefit analysis will help leaders ascertain the highest impact and greatest outcomes for the investment. While educators love a good discount or money-saving deal, the price alone should not be the primary consideration. It's possible that the upfront investment is rather inexpensive, but the long-term commitment to resources is significant—or vice versa. Unless the initiative is intended to terminate by a certain date, a plan for its continued inclusion in the district should be intact.

Consider a district that's ready to revamp its discipline policy due to the lack of discernible behavior corrections using the traditional methods of out-of-class referrals, detention, Saturday school, suspension, and expulsion. Before the team starts making changes, members send out a data chart to all schools to help with their cost-benefit analysis of upholding the current system versus adopting a different one, such as positive behavior intervention and supports (PBIS), with which many other districts have found success. Figure 3.4 (page 50) shows an example of a simple form for collecting and recording data to help the team conduct a cost-benefit analysis of the initiative to develop a new discipline policy.

Once the data has been collected and applied to possible new approaches or programs, the team will critically analyze whether going in a new direction is worthwhile. As you can see, a cost-benefit analysis can take place using historical data to make a determination as well as a format for examining a change in practice for the future. This is the litmus test: How do we maximize the most positive impact for students at the best price? Having a clear understanding of the sought-after outcomes must precede the price consideration. The leader has to be able to articulate how the team will measure impacts to help determine whether it's worth the investment. As indicated in figure 3.5 (page 50), the goal is to aim for the two right-hand quadrants with the highest point values.

Other intangible resources, such as time, energy, and support, are necessary to keep the initiative afloat. These are the hidden factors that truly influence the success of a new plan. It's typical for a lot of excitement to surround a novel idea, but it doesn't take much time for energy to flag. The leader should employ strategies to reinvigorate participants midway through the process. Celebrate successes, however minor they may seem, along the way. Conduct refreshers with reminders of key points. Share data showing progress. Send out memos or short videos highlighting those involved.

School name:		Total	Student	Administrator
		Minutes		
		Hours		
Number of disciplinary actions last year:		Days		

Number of disciplinary actions this year:	
Average number of minutes the student is out of class due to behavior:	
Average number of minutes the administrator needs to process consequences:	

Disaggregated Data:	
Behavior Referrals:	
Attendance or Tardies:	
Suspensions:	
Expulsions:	

Overall Learning Time Lost:	

Costs:	
Benefits:	

Figure 3.4: Discipline policy cost-benefit analysis.

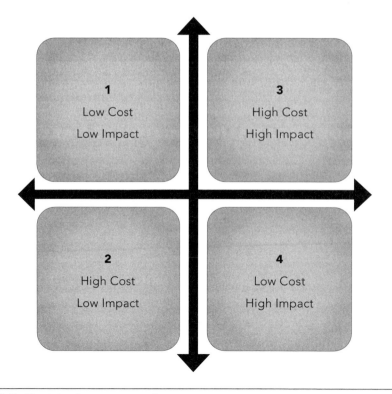

Figure 3.5: Cost-to-impact matrix.

Create incentives for participants. Keep senior management and the board informed. Do whatever you can to remain continually on the radar.

In addition, it's very difficult to accurately predict the amount of time required to root a project into the soil. It's not hyperbole to say that our estimations rarely if ever meet the mark. It *always* takes more time than we originally think. It's always better to under promise and over deliver, so the leader should build in buffers to the timeline that allow for life to happen along the way in the same way they should pad the budget for contingency costs and overruns. Resource management is ongoing, and making adjustments is part of the process. By being as realistic as possible when first prioritizing, both the obvious and the subtle components can work together for success. The value of an initiative also must be communicated and transferred down to those who inherit it beyond the leader's tenure. Otherwise, it will fade not long after that leader walks out the door.

CONCLUSION

The eight criteria delineated in this chapter each play a different role in determining an initiative's overall prioritization. After assigning point values to each one using the "Initiative Prioritization Rubric" (page 52), leaders may still decide to increase the merit of one criterion over another depending on the district's climate, culture, or circumstances. In one locale, impact on learning, timing, and readiness may override strategic alignment and connection to other initiatives. In other places, equity and stakeholder engagement take top billing. Regardless, whether costs and resources can be accommodated for tends to be a universal factor in any institution. Once a new initiative is placed on the prioritization rubric, the initial three stages are complete and the plan moves from theory to action.

STAGE 3 ACTION PLAN: CHECKLIST AND REPRODUCIBLES

The following checklist and reproducibles help you apply what you learned in this chapter and move forward to the next stage of the initiative implementation process.

- ☐ Complete the "Initiative Prioritization Rubric" reproducible (page 52).
- ☐ Complete the "District Plans Crosswalk" reproducible (page 55).
- ☐ Complete the "Cost-Benefit Analysis" reproducible (page 56) for pending initiatives (see figures 3.4 and 3.5, page 50, as models).

Initiative Prioritization Rubric

Directions: List all the initiatives that your school or district is currently considering or recently started. Each team member completes the rubric based on his or her analysis of each criterion for each implementation. Team members then compare their responses with one another and come to consensus on which initiatives should be prioritized over the others. Total agreement is not necessary; the goal is to collectively decide how to prioritize initiatives for the good of the school or district.

1. Write the initiative name at the top of each column.
2. Evaluate each initiative against the first criteria.
3. Using the guiding questions, give each initiative a rating based on how well the initiative fits those criteria.
4. Multiply the weight by your rating.
5. Write the resulting number, the weighted value, in the box for that initiative and criteria.
6. Repeat these steps for each criterion.
7. Add all the values in each of the columns, and write the totals in the boxes at the bottom.

Criteria or Weight	**Rating Scale**	Initiative	Initiative	Initiative
Criteria 1: Strategic Alignment • To what extent is the project aligned with the department or site's vision, mission, and goals? • To what extent is the project aligned with existing frameworks or strategic plans? Weight = ___	1 = Does not align 2 = Some alignment 3 = Full alignment			
Criteria 2: Connection to Other Initiatives • To what degree does the project intersect with or support other district initiatives? • To what degree will the project lay a foundation to support future initiatives? Weight = ___	1 = None; stands alone 2 = Intersects; supports some 3 = Intersects; supports all			

Criteria or Weight	Rating Scale	Initiative	Initiative	Initiative
Criteria 3: Impact on Learning *Consider what the data says about why this initiative is needed.* • To what extent will the project positively impact student learning? • How widespread will the project's impact be across the district? Weight = ___	1 = Low impact 2 = Medium impact 3 = High impact			
Criteria 4: Equity • To what extent will the project increase equity for students? • To what extent does it address the specific, data-driven needs of diverse student groups? Weight = ___	1 = No increase 2 = Some increase 3 = Significant increase			
Criteria 5: Support From Key Stakeholders • What is the level of support from other district office departments (human resources, business, superintendent) or the school board? • What is the level of support from employee associations? • What is the level of support from parents, students, the community at large, or the business community? Weight = ___	1 = Unknown or weak level of support 2 = Support from some 3 = Complete support			

Criteria or Weight	Rating Scale	Initiative	Initiative	Initiative
Criteria 6: Timing and Readiness *Consider the urgency of the problem being solved.* • To what degree is the district ready for this initiative? • To what degree is this the right time for this initiative? Weight = ___	1 = Not ready; too early to tell 2 = Adequately prepared; good timing 3 = Totally prepared; perfect timing			
Criteria 7: Required Service • Is the project required to meet legal, compliance, or regulatory mandates? • Does this project fulfill a moral or ethical obligation? • Is the project responsive to concerns being brought up by staff, students, or parents? Weight = ___	1 = Not required or mandated 2 = Not required but has ethical value 3 = Required or mandated by law			
Criteria 8: Costs and Resources • What is the potential cost-benefit of the project? • What are the other resources, other than money, needed to sustain the effort? Weight = ___	1 = High potential for unknown or unexpected costs 2 = Some costs are known and planned for 3 = All costs, direct and indirect, are known, planned for, and budgeted			
Total Score				

District Plans Crosswalk

Directions: In the left-hand column, list your school or district's focus areas, goals, mission, and vision. Review the various national, state, provincial, and local plans your school or district uses in the remaining columns and indicate which cover the key components you listed in the first column. See figure 3.3 (page 41) for a completed example.

Key Focus Areas *Examples are in italics.*	**Initiative A**	**Initiative B**	**Initiative C**
Ensuring college and career readiness			
Improving graduation rates			
Decreasing chronic absenteeism			
Evaluating programs			
Implementing a multitiered system of supports			
Reducing waste reduction and improving energy efficiency			

Leading the Launch © 2022 Solution Tree Press • SolutionTree.com
Visit **go.SolutionTree.com/leadership** to download this page.

Cost-Benefit Analysis

Directions: Collect all the information you can gather regarding the costs (including time, resources, money, staffing, and materials) for the initiative or initiatives you are planning to implement. Then make a list of the expected benefits for student outcomes. As a leadership team, discuss if there are any additional ways the initiative might be altered to lower costs while increasing impacts before determining a final score in the last box on the chart.

Name of Initiative:	
Potential Costs (select any that apply)	**Expected Benefits** (select any that apply)
1. Fixed monetary costs (for example, hardware, materials, textbooks) Rank (circle one): high or low	1. Student achievement (for example, standardized test scores, language acquisition fluency rates, graduation rates) Rank (circle one): high or low
2. Variable monetary costs (for example, training, consumables, licensing or annual fees) Rank (circle one): high or low	2. Family engagement (for example, parent attendance at school events, responses to communications, clicks on website) Rank (circle one): high or low
3. Human resource or staffing Rank (circle one): high or low	3. School culture and safety (for example, fewer accident reports, higher marks on climate survey, reduction in disciplinary referrals) Rank (circle one): high or low
4. Time investment Rank (circle one): high or low	4. Local metrics (for example, school-based incentive programs, report cards, attendance rates) Rank (circle one): high or low
5. Other costs (for example, communications, information) Rank (circle one): high or low	5. Additional benefits Rank (circle one): high or low
6. Cost savings Rank (circle one): high or low	
Overall placement determination on matrix: 1 2 3 4	

CHAPTER 4

Stage 4: Design the Proof of Concept, Prototype, and Pilot

Now comes the fun part! It's time to move from talk to action. At this stage, you will discover how your inspiration and ideas play out in real time. Think about playing in a sandbox filled with all kinds of tools and building instruments and letting your imagination run wild. More often than not, the reality of creating the exact image that's in your mind doesn't turn out perfectly the first, second, or even third time. There are fits and starts, collapses and reconstruction, and trials and errors to help you refine your decision making and learn from what does and doesn't work.

In essence, you can adapt and apply the four critical questions of a PLC discussed in chapter 3 (DuFour et al., 2016) to guide this process along the way.

1. What do we want to learn by conducting this pilot?
2. How will we know if we've learned what we need to proceed?
3. What will we do to intervene when it's not going well?
4. What will we do to expand on early successes?

This chapter explores the elements of design leading up to launching a pilot. While the very nature of the activities in this stage can feel ambiguous or inexact, that's the point. They are meant to challenge your original assumptions to see if they hold true and allow you to reshape your approach through new realizations. Prior to piloting, the leadership team will formulate a blueprint for action including developing a proof of concept, testing out the concept in a prototype model, and expanding the prototype into a more robust trial pilot period.

BLUEPRINT FOR ACTION

Synthesizing the information gathered in stages 2 and 3 will form the blueprint for action. A *proof of concept* is a brief exercise to test the idea or initiative, while a *prototype* is a preliminary model or simulation built to test that concept or process. Once the prototype proves potentially worthy, it can be launched into a pilot. This involves outlining the *who*, *what*, *when*, *where*, *why*, and *how* of the initiative. A pilot tests out the new initiative on a limited scale to identify its strengths, weaknesses, gaps, and opportunities. Figure 4.1 illustrates how the steps build progress.

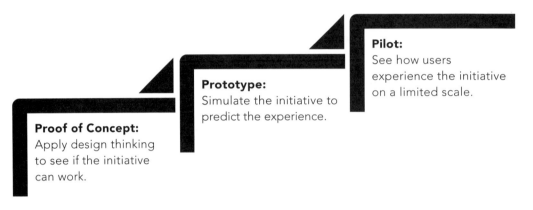

Figure 4.1: Blueprint for action: proof of concept, prototype, and pilot.

*Visit **go.SolutionTree.com/leadership** for a free reproducible version of this figure.*

PROOF OF CONCEPT THROUGH DESIGN THINKING

Design has traditionally been associated with art, architecture, clothing, furnishings, and other visually creative endeavors. However, design thinking has expanded that concept to incorporate other industries such as education, social services, user experiences, and innovative processes. Simply defined, *design thinking* is a human-centered approach to problem solving modern-day dilemmas or enhancing lives. According to Lor's (2017) critical literature review on design thinking in the educational arena:

> In short, design thinking uses the sensibilities or mindsets and methodologies often used by designers to create new ideas, solutions, alternatives and choices that satisfy the desires of the end users or stakeholders. . . . Design thinking, as a holistic concept to design cognition and learning, allows the participants to work successfully in multi-disciplinary teams as they creatively solve difficult real-life problems. (as cited in Rauth, Köppen, Jobst, & Meinel, 2010, pp. 41–42)

Design thinking can serve as the first step in the building blocks by fleshing out your proof of concept on the road to executing your pilot. Lor (2017) states: "The whole idea is to fail, and fail fast, in order to learn from the failures and rapidly iterate in order not to miss opportunities and waste resources" (p. 43).

The unique idea behind this approach is that it's rooted in a place of empathy—one begins by imagining the ideal benefits for the people it will touch. Tim Brown, CEO of the innovative think tank IDEO (Brown & Wyatt, 2010), was an early creator of the concept that high-impact solutions to social problems bubble up from below rather than being imposed from the top through the three intersecting spaces of inspiration, ideation, and implementation. In the case of district initiatives, the focus must lie squarely on students. That does not mean an initiative that serves adults, such as families or employees, is of lesser importance. But the bottom line should be that any project that is one dimension away from direct service to students ultimately needs to have a positive effect on them as well.

Adopting an online attendance system, refurbishing an administration office, developing a volunteer handbook, changing the bell schedule, or creating a policy for parking lot drop off and pick up are all primarily adult-oriented. At their center, however, are the students. Will the new attendance system penalize students whose parents are the root cause for their tardiness? Does the volunteer handbook contain clauses for removing volunteers who interact negatively with students? Does the bell schedule take into account leaving enough time for restroom use, play, or nutrition? Questions like these, that go beyond the logistics, are necessary to ensure that youth development, safety, security, and educational support are at the core of designing new initiatives.

THE PROTOTYPE

After the proof of concept has been deemed viable, the leadership team moves into prototyping. Now your conceptual design evolves into a practical approach by fleshing out the details and determining how to apply it to a particular setting. The essential goal of prototyping is to spell out how a new initiative may look in a field test. The prototype is intended to be malleable and responsive to stakeholders' reactions and feedback. The following case study demonstrates how a prototype process might unfold.

CASE STUDY

Weekly Collaboration Hour for Teachers (the Prototype)

Hamilton High, an urban high school, votes to alter the bell schedule to incorporate a weekly collaboration hour for teachers. The current schedule allows for monthly staff and department meetings, but no formal time for teachers to collaborate. The goal is to allow time for teachers to work together on lesson planning, assessment development, interventions, and extension activities.

The heart of this release time is for instructors to reflect on their practice and build their skill sets to improve student learning.

In addition to the collaboration time, they want to incorporate a twice-per-week flex period for students. This flex time has a dual purpose. Students can sign up for extra academic support for specific classes in which they are struggling. Or, they can choose to take enrichment courses such as yoga, tinker with found objects in a maker's space, or meet up in the wellness center for a group counseling session. Flex time is intended to break up the monotony of the current traditional six-period day and enrich student life at the school.

Incorporating both of these ideas into the bell schedule is simultaneously exciting and daunting. If done well, these two changes can uplift the entire school environment. Teachers learn best practices from each other, reinvigorate their curriculum, and make better data-informed decisions in the classroom. Students get some extended time to grasp difficult concepts in a small-group setting or can spend time participating in engaging activities or innovative ideas.

One of the comprehensive high school principals in the district is ready to take on the pilot and report back. Staff, parents, and students alike seem enthusiastic about trying out the schedule for the second semester of the school year. The principal meets with the superintendent and senior cabinet to get all her ducks in a row. At the meeting, she shares the draft schedule to make sure that it meets the proper number of required instructional minutes and doesn't violate any contractual obligations. She also presents them with a chart answering the *who*, *what*, *when*, *where*, *why*, and *how* of the pilot plan (see figure 4.2). Satisfied that the plan covers all bases, permission is granted to design the pilot.

Bell Schedule Pilot Plan for Hamilton High School	
Who will participate in the pilot?	110 teachers and 2,300 students
What are the participants' expectations?	<ul><li>Teachers will collaborate weekly in their content area departments for one hour.</li><li>Teachers will document their collaboration topics and meeting minutes in a shared drive.</li><li>Teachers will offer academic support and enrichment activities for students during flex time.</li><li>Students will use the online sign-up app each morning on flex days for the courses they plan to attend.</li><li>Students will scan their ID cards at their flex location and attend the entire forty-minute session.</li></ul>
When will the pilot take place?	Spring semester (January–June)
Where are the most appropriate locations to try out the initiative?	<ul><li>The location will be one of the eight comprehensive high schools in the district.</li><li>Hamilton High is an appropriate location because the staff, students, and parents are already on board with the idea.</li></ul>

Why is this good for students?	Students will benefit significantly from the following. • Teachers collaborate together and reflect on what they are doing in the classroom to improve instruction. • They have time for extra help with their academic work. • They are exposed to a variety of learning opportunities. • They have a late start time once a week for extra sleep. • They receive a break in the middle of the day, two times per week. • They experience increased engagement and connections with different teachers and students during flex time. • They can catch up on missed work or tests due to absences.
How will the initiative be introduced, communicated, and rolled out?	• Prior to winter break, send home a letter to students' families, explaining the new schedule. • Hold family or parent forums to field questions or concerns. • Issue students' new schedules in January with the late-start Wednesday and the Tuesday and Thursday flex times included. • In homeroom, show students how to download the flex-time app on their devices or cell phones to book classes. • In the first week, everyone will do a dry run of the schedule to see if there are any glitches to work out. • Students and teachers will debrief the following week and make any necessary adjustments. • Nine weeks in, at the quarter break, administer a survey to students, parents, and staff to assess how the pilot is going. • Administration will review the data and see if mid-semester changes need to take place. • At the end of the school year, the administration and counseling staff will analyze the course sign-ups to find out the most popular options students selected from the app. • The principal will share the outcomes with the other principals and senior management with a recommendation to continue the pilot, launch the implementation full-scale, or discontinue it entirely.

Figure 4.2: Bell schedule pilot plan for Hamilton High School.

While prototyping is predominantly a mental exercise, it also treads lightly into real-world application to determine if pursuing a pilot is feasible. Some aspects of the prototype may be included in the next iteration, but it's also possible that the pilot may be significantly different depending on the outcomes the prototype yields.

THE PILOT

Care and feeding during the pilot period are essential. Neglecting to pay keen attention to the factors in motion leaves too much to chance, thus making it difficult to tease out which intentional actions made it a success or failure versus what was merely happenstance. It can be tempting to swerve left or right when something is not going well, but troubleshooting requires isolating the likely responsible variables and addressing them one by one.

The four critical questions of a PLC (as modified for the piloting phase) will help you stay on track by establishing your learning objectives up front, assessing how it's going via collecting qualitative or quantitative data, and correcting the course or capitalizing on advancements as they unfold. Your team can complete the "Four Critical Questions for the Pilot" reproducible (page 66) to help guide you through the pilot.

Management by walking around, observing, and engaging in impromptu conversations is a great strategy for taking the pulse of how a pilot is going. One way to gather solid input is to witness how things are working on the ground. Seeing is believing—the flaws become glaring; the highlights will shine.

CASE STUDY

Weekly Collaboration Hour for Teachers (the Pilot)

Returning to the previous scenario at Hamilton High School, the principal spends the first two weeks of the pilot visiting the flex periods to see which are most popularly attended, and popping into the teachers' collaboration sessions for brief observations. By taking this dipstick approach, she can quickly synthesize key themes and identify potential problems with the schedule change.

She discovers that the schedule itself is working logistically quite well. The students, parents, and teachers have adjusted their timetables accordingly, and everyone is in the right places at the right times. However, the content of both the flex period sessions and the teacher collaboration meetings vary widely in substance and efficacy.

On the low-functioning end, some of the flex periods resemble a traditional study hall without much interaction between instructors and students; likewise, some department meetings are consumed with textbook checkout coordination, copy paper ordering, and other menial tasks. On the high-functioning end, the flex periods bustle with active engagement between staff and students, and the most appealing topics' waitlists are overflowing. Several teacher teams are intensively delving into the most recent formative assessment data and working on remediation and enrichment lessons for small-group instruction the following day, while others are coordinating recess duty and scheduling computer lab time.

Differentiation is fundamental. As referenced earlier, we must isolate the variables that need intervention, while at the same time reinforcing the conditions for those that are already thriving. Just as with classroom instruction, "one size fits all" does not work. Therefore, the principal takes a multi-pronged approach to determine whether skill or will are the predominant issues with the flex options or the collaboration time. Since both are novel concepts, she may need to lay some more groundwork with information, professional development, or mentoring to bolster the groups that are flailing. It may simply be that they don't know how to structure the periods effectively or understand what the content should include.

Figure 4.3 is one of the tools the principal can use to review how teachers believe the pilot is going.

We launch pilot programs so we can learn from them and adapt the program prior to full-scale implementation. Our school's instructional leadership team (ILT) wants to hear from you! Your responses will remain confidential and anonymous, so please share your honest feedback so we can work together and get it right! For each item, please place a checkmark in the column that best describes your experiences so far.

Part 1: How's it going?

As result of this pilot, so far . . .	Low	Medium	High
My knowledge has increased.			
My attitude has evolved.			
My skills and abilities have improved.			
My instructional planning has deepened.			
The way I teach has expanded.			
The way I monitor progress has expanded.			
My relationships with students have improved.			
My relationships with colleagues have improved.			
I am more willing to take instructional risks.			
My students are more engaged and participatory.			
I am more satisfied with my job performance.			

Part 2: What do you need?

Going forward . . .	Low	Medium	High
I need more training on how to use the online tools.			
I need more content knowledge.			
I need more collaboration time with my team.			
I need to learn additional instructional strategies.			
I need to find new ways to assess progress.			
I need ideas for intervention and extension groupings.			

Figure 4.3: Mid-pilot process check.   continued ▶

Going forward . . .	Low	Medium	High
I need some activities for community building.			
I need some strategies to increase participation.			
I need a better variety of materials to work with.			
I need support communicating learning objectives with parents.			
I need an easy-to-use planning template.			
I need more direct feedback on my teaching.			

Based on the results of the process check, during week four, the principal at Hamilton High switches things up. Instead of individual departments meeting for collaboration time, she arranges for the entire staff to do a fishbowl exercise to observe two highly functioning groups working together. Then the whole staff debriefs and discusses ways to capitalize on the time they've been given.

At the end of the meeting, the principal also provides anyone the choice to forgo their own flex period the following week and pair up with another teacher they want to learn from in refining their own offerings. By treating these as learning opportunities, she creates a nonthreatening environment in which people can take risks and bounce back from missteps with both dignity and increased dexterity.

Vulnerable and flexible leadership includes acknowledging errors in judgment and making necessary adjustments. Maintaining a growth mindset is critical in the prototype and piloting phases. Failure should not only be expectedbut also required. No pilot ever works perfectly out of the gate. Instead of feeling frustrated at the inevitable flubs and flaws, a leader with an open mind embraces this information as a natural part of the feedback loop. Not only does this provide an excellent role model for staff, but it also walks the talk for students, too.

CONCLUSION

The collective power of the three Ps—proof of concept, prototype, and pilot—command center stage in this part of the process. What is gleaned, gathered, and grappled with during this experimental phase brings what was once fuzzy into clearer focus and allows the leadership team to plan their next concrete steps. The "fast fails" (Lor, 2017) present several lessons to learn from and anticipate when it comes to the next steps in the new initiative process. If anything summarizes stage 4 best, it is comprised of a series of "trials and errors" to separate the wheat from the chaff.

Concurrently with conducting any experiment, communication plays a significant role, which leads us into the next stage—stakeholder engagement. Stage 5 is not as linear as the others, and there is much merit to beginning it concurrently with stage 4. Prior to the pilot launch, the leader prepares a comprehensive list of stakeholders to ask for input, including advisory committees, councils, employee associations, the school district's board of trustees, parent or community groups, students, and so on.

Even if it doesn't directly affect them, those running the pilot will share what's happening with all site principals and other district office departments, so they can be allies and advocates in the face of opposition or help to quell the rumor mill. By selecting dates, reserving rooms, and creating assessment tools in advance, people know that their input is welcomed, valued, and used to refine the implementation. You will learn more about how this works in chapter 5 (page 69).

STAGE 4 ACTION PLAN: CHECKLIST AND REPRODUCIBLES

The following checklist and reproducibles help you apply what you learned in this chapter and move forward to the next stage of the initiative implementation process.

- ☐ Design the proof of concept, prototype, and pilot framework (see figure 4.1, page 58).
- ☐ Complete the "Four Critical Questions for the Pilot" reproducible (page 66).
- ☐ Complete the "Mid-Pilot Process Check" reproducible (page 67).

Four Critical Questions for the Pilot

Directions: Use this planning template with your leadership team to prepare for piloting the new initiative. Fill out the right column individually or as a whole team and come to consensus on your responses to ensure clarity. Refer back to it throughout stage 4 to help you proceed through the challenges and make adjustments accordingly.

Critical Question	Responses
1. What do we want to learn by conducting this pilot?	Our goals and intentions behind this pilot are:
	We hope to learn:
2. How will we know if we've learned what we need to proceed?	We will use the following formative assessments to collect data:
	We will analyze the data using these methods:
3. What will we do to intervene when it's not going well?	We will look for these indicators that interventions may be needed:
	Our intervention plan will include these possible strategies:
4. What will we do to expand on early successes?	We will look for these indicators that we are exceeding our original goals:
	Our expansion plans will include these possible strategies:

Mid-Pilot Process Check

Directions: We are seeking your feedback on how the _____ pilot is going, so the leadership team can make the necessary adjustments for the second half of the school year. For Part 1, rate each criterion regarding your experiences with the pilot at this point in time. For Part 2, rate each criterion regarding what you think is needed to improve the pilot process for the future.

Part 1: As result of this pilot so far . . .	Low	Medium	High
My knowledge base . . .			
My attitude has . . .			
My skills and abilities are . . .			
I am more willing to . . .			
The way I work has . . .			
My students are . . .			
My relationships have . . .			
I am more satisfied with . . .			
I am curious about . . .			
I am struggling with . . .			

Part 2: Going forward . . .	Low	Medium	High
I need to understand . . .			
I want more . . .			
We should stop doing . . .			
We should start doing . . .			
I want to find ways to . . .			
I need ideas for . . .			
I need some activities for . . .			
I need some strategies to . . .			
I need a variety of materials related to . . .			
I need support in developing . . .			

CHAPTER 5

Stage 5: Build Stakeholder Engagement

There is no more vital or demanding stage than building authentic stakeholder engagement. Although the first four stages in the new initiative process yield their own set of challenges, once the initiative hits the street, the street is going to react. That feedback must be funneled in a productive direction, or we risk letting it run amuck.

Engagement is one of those terms we use a lot in the field of education, although its definition is rather loose, depending on the context. For our purposes, we will use the definition: getting to know your stakeholders' values, interests, and perspectives; soliciting their input; and shaping decision making around their contributions. This definition heavily emphasizes three main attributes: (1) engaging in authentic two-way interaction with and between multiple audiences, (2) considering all feedback (even if not incorporated in the final product), and (3) sharing all major decisions with stakeholders.

This chapter presents how to identify your stakeholders and use various modes of outreach, manage expectations, and bounce back from pitfalls that can occur even when we have the best of intentions.

STAKEHOLDER GROUPS

Conscientiously defining who your stakeholders are in advance accomplishes several goals: (1) it keeps your focus in the right direction and serves as a reminder to the leadership team that the initiative is not about us, but about our stakeholders; (2) it ensures diversity of voice and perspective, which will result in richer feedback to act on, and; (3) it creates wider-spread familiarity with the initiative so it doesn't seem like it comes from out of the blue when eventually launched.

As shown in figure 5.1, there are concentric circles of influence to consider: the end user or consumer, of course, is at the middle of the bullseye, but let's not forget to include the outer orbiters as well. At times, those not at the center need to be brought into the fold even more, as they don't have the central experience and may be relying on hearsay or incomplete observations. You will have an opportunity to replicate the model and apply it to your own circumstances in the action planning section at the end of this chapter.

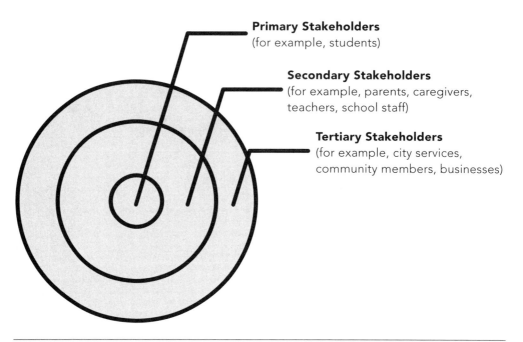

Figure 5.1: Circles of influence.

When beginning to craft your engagement plan, these probing questions can help you cover most bases embodied in the circle of influence.

- Who are the primary stakeholders, end users, or direct recipients of the new initiative? Name specific groups or subgroups at the center of the implementation.

- Who are the secondary stakeholders in the school or district that may be impacted by the implementation? Think about the people one or two degrees away from the center of the initiative and how they might interface with or react to it.

- Who are the tertiary stakeholders that the initiative actually may not touch but should be informed as a courtesy, such as the city council, the Parent Teacher Association (PTA), employee associations, or the local chamber of commerce?

- Now go back and ask, "Who did we forget?" and "Where do they fit?" Repeat until all possible groups or individuals are accounted for.
- Your final consideration for the invisible outermost rung on the circle is not included in figure 5.1 but could be a factor. If the initiative is potentially controversial or there are political dynamics at play, it may spur viral national or social media attention. Anticipate your critics' arguments and be ready to respond with facts, positive messaging, press releases, and frequently asked questions (FAQs) to head them off at the pass.

THE Cs OF COMMUNICATION

Engagement is multifaceted. Communication is nuanced. Owen Hargie's (2011) research on interpersonal communications identifies three core types of psychological needs that we should be aware of when designing our outreach efforts: competence, relatedness, and autonomy. Hargie (2011) states:

> The competence need involves a wish to feel confident and effective in carrying out actions, in order to achieve one's goals. The relatedness need reflects a desire to have close connections and positive relationships with significant others. The autonomy need involves wanting to feel in control of one's own destiny, rather than being directed by others. (p. 2)

Since perception can often be perceived as reality, tending to people's psychological needs is paramount. While some people truly enjoy novelty and exploring uncharted territories, many tread more lightly and keep a wary eye out for danger signs. A leadership team can help people feel safer employing communication strategies that reduce unintended stressors and foster a sense of belonging.

Employing one or all of the following communication methods may be appropriate at any given time to meet one or more of the participants' needs.

- **Correspond:** Send out messages, emails, flyers, or newsletters to inform stakeholders about details of the initiative, meeting dates and times, or next steps.
- **Collaborate:** Brainstorm ideas, novel approaches, or problem-solving techniques with team members.
- **Come to consensus:** Distill ideas from the think tank and agree on the best ones.
- **Contribute:** Solicit data, information, and suggestions for improving the pilot phase.

- **Consult:** Find experts in the field on the topic to share insights, professional opinions, and guidance on moving the initiative forward.
- **Correlate:** Explicitly link the initiative to work already being done at the district or site so people can connect the dots.
- **Compromise:** Make concessions for what's not working and change up the original strategy to remove unnecessary stumbling blocks.
- **Calibrate:** Bring external factors into account or compare with other data, then make corrections as needed.
- **Check-in:** Visit, touch base, inquire, poll, survey, dialogue, take the temperature, and observe what's going on using all of the faculties at your disposal.
- **Confess:** Cop to any errors in judgment or execution along the way, whether made inadvertently or not.
- **Commit:** Pledge resources, support, or whatever else is needed to promote the project's long-term success.
- **Circulate:** Share widely between and beyond stakeholder groups to publicize the initiative. Blanket the site or district with information via social media, sound bites, and word of mouth to expand outreach.
- **Conclude:** Once input has been gathered, summarize the responses, agreements, and action steps, and circle back to those who participated in the outreach.
- **Carry-through:** Keep promises.

This is not an exhaustive list of communication methods, but it serves as a menu of options. The key is flexibility. By staying mentally nimble, the leader can switch up the technique as the situation demands. If the feedback isn't getting at the core of what's being sought, we then change tactics. It may take a few attempts, but all information gathered from any course of action can prove useful.

A PLAN FOR OUTREACH

Getting the right ingredients to increase parent involvement at school has been widely discussed in the educational arena for decades. National organizations, such as the PTA and local educational foundations, have worked tirelessly to bridge communications between the community and the system. School administrators have been equally in search of best practices to encourage higher engagement. Typically, schools have a small percentage of frequent attendees who sign up for every committee, fill out every survey, and attend every board meeting. A much larger group in the middle may read the school newsletter, visit the district website, and participate only when the topic personally affects them. And then there is an undeterminable number of people who don't engage at all for all kinds of reasons, ranging from they trust the system and that the decision makers will do their jobs to they don't have time, energy, or know how to access information that may impact their family.

There is no one right method, but by applying the theory of Abraham Maslow's (1943, 1954) hierarchy of human needs to your toolkit, you can deliberately accommodate diverse needs as well as break down the barriers that can keep a wider variety of people from showing up. In his research, Maslow developed a hierarchy, usually presented as a pyramid, with the most basic needs at the bottom: (1) physiological, (2) safety, (3) belonging, and (4) esteem. Individuals must meet these first four needs before moving on to the final one, which relates to personal growth: (5) self-actualization. Figure 5.2 shows these needs on a ladder to help visualize the five levels in the hierarchy.

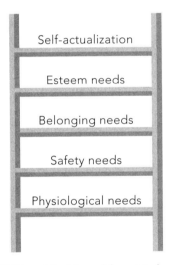

Source: Adapted from Boogren, 2018, p. 17; Adapted from Maslow, 1943, 1971.

Figure 5.2: Maslow's hierarchy of needs.

Figure 5.3 (page 74) aligns the five levels of Maslow's hierarchy of needs to strategies leaders should consciously employ when setting up their campaign. Though the Maslow pyramid has been updated into many other iterations since 1943, for our purposes, the original version captures the primary building blocks for designing a strong communications plan. The left column contains the title and a key tenet that illustrates that particular need. The right column offers suggestions to help leadership teams carefully consider the experience from their stakeholders' viewpoints and mindsets.

Maslow's Hierarchy of Needs	Strategies for Family and Community Engagement
Level 5: Self-Actualization Tenet: Achieving Potential or Mastery	Explain the purpose of the outreach. Deliver on expectations and outcomes. Give participants an active role. Personalize the experience. Address them as experts and professionals. Present them with a problem to solve. Utilize their knowledge and skills sets. Assign them high-level critical thinking tasks.
Level 4: Self-Esteem Tenet: Acceptance	Use inclusive language; gently correct unintentional stereotyping or bias from others. Honor all cultures, languages, and background experiences. Validate their suggestions. Differentiate instruction for a range of participants. Offer praise to encourage discussion. Respect their involvement by starting and ending on time. Check for understanding periodically. Have the participants set and commit to norms.
Level 3: Love and Belonging Tenet: Relationships	Send personalized invitations or make phone calls. Coordinate volunteers to guide people from parking lot to meeting space. Put out ample welcome and directional signs, and greet participants at the door. Arrange tables and chairs to boost interactions. Do an easy icebreaker to build a feeling of community. Set the tone with a smile, anecdote, or personal story. Be aware of cultural diversity when planning group activities. Encourage them to work in collaborative teams.
Level 2: Safety Tenet: Comfort	Set heat and air conditioning to moderate temperatures. Have lights on for evening meetings. Select a convenient, centralized location. Ensure accessibility for people with disabilities or special needs.

	Make sure there is more than enough (and a variety of) seating options.
	Provide restroom and socializing breaks.
	Prearrange for translation services (for example, someone to translate in American Sign Language [ASL]; someone to translate into the top two languages other than English).
	Explain any confidentiality ground rules up front.
	Use familiar (social media, text messaging) modes of communication with sufficient and accurate details.
Level 1: Physiological Well-Being Tenet: Food, Shelter, Health	Provide onsite child care with trusted staff.
	Have snacks or meals available.
	Offer transportation options (for example, transit maps, tickets, free parking).
	Make arrangements for inclement weather (for example, an alternative indoor location).
	Go to them (for example, community center, apartment complex courtyard, religious institutions).
	Stagger meeting times to accommodate caregivers' various work schedules.
	Send home appropriate takeaways or door prizes.

Source: Adapted from Maslow, 1943, 1971.

Figure 5.3: Maslow's hierarchy outreach strategies.

ONE SIZE DOES NOT FIT ALL

There is much truth to the saying that everyone's a critic, especially with an unfamiliar concept or experience. Our human nature is to be wary of change, and our latent animal nature may actively bare its teeth against it. Therefore, planning how to respond to resistance and address misinformation is essential. We should continue to heed Maslow's hierarchy of needs in this stage in order to more accurately interpret the feedback we receive. Regardless of the rank on the pyramid, it can be easy to mistake negative commentary for something being wrong with the initiative; it may, instead, be a reaction to an unmet need. The following case study illustrates this concept.

CASE STUDY

After-School Tutoring Program

Seashore Middle School is piloting an after-school tutoring program. University students can earn course credit for volunteering their time for homework support between 3:00–6:00 p.m. Seventh and eighth graders are referred by the school staff, and their parents are consulted for consent. Although students are the direct customers, so to speak, their parents and teachers are also at the crux of the initiative. Happy children may influence, but do not necessarily equate to, happy adults. The students in the homework club may appear to enjoy and benefit from it, but we also need to see if the hoped-for outcomes are reaching families and teachers.

Six weeks into the pilot, the principal distributes exit slips to parents and families at pick-up time. The three-question prompt asks parents the following.

- Has the tutoring improved your child's grades?
- Are the tutors helping your child learn the course content?
- Would you have your child continue the program if we offered it as an ongoing option?

The students are asked similar questions geared toward their own experiences in the tutoring program. The instruction leadership team at the school then reviews the collective comments. Each content area department chair plus the principal, assistant principal, and counselors measure the feedback based on Maslow's hierarchy to filter the open-ended responses.

Figure 5.4 shows a sampling of student comments.

Need	Positive Response (Met)	Negative Response (Unmet)
Self-Actualization	"I met my goal." "Oh, I see it now." "I am getting As on my tests."	"I just can't do it." "I don't get it." "I'm not learning anything."
Self-Esteem	"I feel excited or energized." "I'm smart."	"I feel depressed or frustrated." "I'm dumb."
Love and Belonging	"I am happy to be with my friends in this program." "The college students make tutoring fun!"	"No one understands me here." "Why do I have to come here when none of my friends do?"
Safety	"I like having a place to go before my parents come home at night." "My tutors are friendly and nice to me."	"My friends make fun of me for having to come here." "I feel like I'm in jail."
Physiological Well-Being	"Tutoring saves me time at night." "I can concentrate on getting my homework done in a quiet place."	"I'm too tired to go to more school." "I am worried about not helping my family out at home while I'm here."

Figure 5.4: Student feedback about after-school tutoring pilot program.

Students' reactions are rooted in personal experience and may glaringly differ from their parents' points of view on the same topic. It is not uncommon that a middle schooler's social-emotional desire for autonomy conflicts with her mother's urge to keep her focused on academics. The tween would much rather be hanging out with friends after school than attending tutoring, thus she proclaims that the after-school program is boring or stupid. Conversely, her mother is thrilled that there is a safe place for her daughter to finish her homework until she can pick her up from school. She also notes an increase in homework completion and corresponding improvement in her child's grades. Both reactions are true and valid. Mitigating between them is a leadership opportunity.

Perception is reality when it comes to stakeholder outreach and input. And it's important to recognize that perception is often more about feelings than rationality. Emotions are mutable, however, and shaped by circumstance. Creating the conditions for helping people sort through their own reactions can help uncover what's beneath the tip of the iceberg of their outward expression. There are many ways to approach these opportunities, including holding small focus groups with guided questions, conducting one-on-one conversations, sending out surveys, or doing listening tours (in which the audience has an open forum to share their ideas without interruption from the leader). The only truly wrong way to do engagement is to not do it at all; with the caveat, however, that it's genuine. If the audience perceives that a conclusion is already foregone, they will lose faith in the leader and the initiative.

Stakeholder engagement is about managing risk and expectations. Much can be gleaned from the participants based on their reactions to the trial phase of the initiative. By categorizing the responses into groups of influencers that should be kept satisfied, observed closely, frequently informed, or convinced of the value of the initiative, we can tailor next steps in the process. The relationships formed during this collaborative stage are critical to advancing the project on a wider scale when the time comes. When people feel that they are contributing to something larger than themselves, they become more invested in its success.

Asking for and digesting honest feedback is harder than it appears. When our hearts and minds are invested in a project, we really want to see it succeed. So anything that feels critical or even less than enthusiastic can be ego-bruising. We must resist the urge to get defensive. This may come in the form of starting to answer peoples' questions before they've even finished asking them, cutting someone off mid-statement, or tossing out criticisms. Maintaining a cool demeanor that's unattached to an outcome is a tall order, but one that serves us well. Because if we don't heed the warning signs at this stage, they will come back to haunt us down the road.

Finally, we want to be aware of power dynamics and trust in the outreach phase. Consider the roles we hold and the people in relationship to them. Kelly Bates, Cynthia Parker, and Curtis Ogden (2018) state that:

> Power—the capacity to get things done—is neither positive nor negative in and of itself. It's all about how we construct, reconstruct, and practice

> power. Individuals can exercise their power in healthy ways if they stay focused on making space for others and growing power to achieve positive outcomes by building 'power with' others. Individuals and groups can exercise their power in unhealthy ways if they are focused on establishing 'power over' others or concentrating power in a few.

When asking colleagues their opinions about a project, leaders must be cognizant that these individuals may say what they think the leader wants to hear, not how they really feel. Even offering the opportunity to send in anonymous feedback can create suspicion that the responses are being electronically tracked and can be traced back to the sender. Sometimes naming the elephant in the room can expose people's core fears and lower their affective filter. Creating as safe an atmosphere as possible is crucial when it comes to minimizing underlying forces that constrain honesty.

When a situation starts to go south, as it can without warning (for example, you notice body language becoming defensive, side conversations cropping up, or outright refusal to participate), you may possibly avert disaster by shifting the power. The leader can use humanizing, nonthreatening sentence frames such as the following.

- "I don't think I communicated that very clearly. Let me try again."
- "I get a sense of frustration in the room. Let me see if I understand what it's about. And if I'm wrong, please correct me."
- "Let's take a quick break so you can give me some feedback about how you're feeling so far."
- "If you were in my shoes, what would you want me to know from your perspective?"
- And the granddaddy of them all: "Wait. I made a mistake. I apologize for . . . ."

Asking for and acting on results is essential to offset the power dynamics as well as elicit truthful feedback. Remember that this is about them, not about you.

CONCLUSION

The bottom line is that stakeholders should have a say in decisions that affect their lives or environment. Also, their participation must include assurances that their contributions will influence upcoming actions and eventual implementation. Not that they will get everything they want; but that they will see the will of the majority reflected in the outcome. Lastly, they should have a role in designing how they partake in the feedback loop. Two-way communication works, and leaders who actively seek out authentic input will undoubtedly end up with an overall better product, service, or procedure. Stakeholder engagement is sometimes messy and unpredictable, but when paired with data collection and analysis in the next stage, it will develop what may currently seem like a blurry photo into a sharper image.

STAGE 5 ACTION PLAN: CHECKLIST AND REPRODUCIBLES

The following checklist and reproducibles help you apply what you learned in this chapter and move forward to the next stage of the initiative implementation process.

- ☐ Define your stakeholder groups by completing the "Stakeholder Groups" reproducible (page 80).

- ☐ Select the most appropriate or applicable communications options from the Cs of Communication (pages 71–72) to plan your multi-pronged outreach strategies.

- ☐ Test Maslow's hierarchy of needs against your chosen engagement strategies using the "Maslow's Hierarchy of Needs Analysis" reproducible (page 83).

Stakeholder Groups

Directions: Answer the questions in section I and then identify the specific names of key leaders, organizations, contact information, and methods for reaching out to your stakeholders in section II.

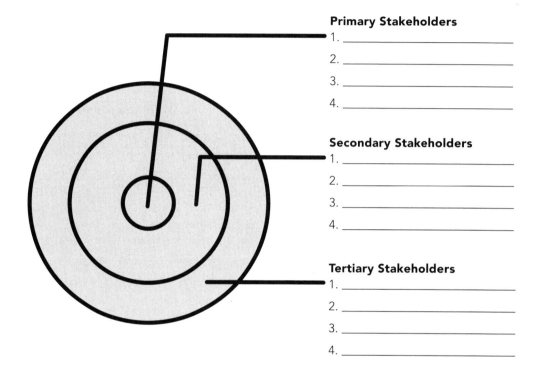

Primary Stakeholders
1. _____
2. _____
3. _____
4. _____

Secondary Stakeholders
1. _____
2. _____
3. _____
4. _____

Tertiary Stakeholders
1. _____
2. _____
3. _____
4. _____

Section I:

Planning Questions	Leadership Team Response
Who are the primary stakeholders, end users, or direct recipients of the new initiative? Name specific groups or subgroups at the center of the implementation.	
Who are the secondary stakeholders in the school or district who may be impacted by the implementation? Think about the people one or two degrees away from the center of the initiative and how they might interface with or react to it.	
Who are the tertiary stakeholders who the initiative actually may not touch but should be informed as a courtesy (for example, city council, the PTA, employee associations)?	
Now go back and ask, "Who did we forget?" and "Where do they fit?" Repeat until all possible groups or individuals are accounted for.	

Section II:

Primary Stakeholders

Name	Organization	Contact Information	Method of Outreach

Secondary Stakeholders

Name	Organization	Contact Information	Method of Outreach

Tertiary Stakeholders

Name	Organization	Contact Information	Method of Outreach

Leading the Launch © 2022 Solution Tree Press • SolutionTree.com
Visit **go.SolutionTree.com/leadership** to download this page.

Maslow's Hierarchy of Needs Analysis

Directions: When planning your outreach strategies, consider the following levels of Maslow's hierarchy of needs to enhance participation at all five tiers of engagement:

Maslow's Hierarchy of Needs	Guiding Questions for Family and Community Engagement
Level 5: Self-Actualization Tenet: Achieving Potential or Mastery	What is the purpose of the outreach? What are the expectations and outcomes of the session? What roles will participants play? How will we personalize the experience? What type of problems will we pose for them to solve? How can we best utilize participants' knowledge and skills sets?
Level 4: Self-Esteem Tenet: Acceptance	How will we encourage use of inclusive language or correct unintentional stereotyping or bias from others? In what ways can we honor all cultures, languages, and background experiences? What are some strategies we can embed to validate participants' suggestions? How might we differentiate instruction for a range of participants? What are some ways to periodically check for understanding? What kind of process will we use to set and maintain norms?
Level 3: Love and Belonging Tenet: Relationships	Who will be assigned to personalize invitations or make phone calls? Who can we tap as volunteers to guide people from parking lot to meeting space? Who will be responsible for setting out welcome and directional signs and greet participants at the door? How might we arrange tables and chairs to boost interactions? What would be a good icebreaker to build a sense of community that is inclusive of cultural, social, and linguistic diversity? What guidelines should we suggest for when participants are asked to collaborate in teams?

Maslow's Hierarchy of Needs	Guiding Questions for Family and Community Engagement
Level 2: Safety Tenet: Comfort	Assign someone to coordinate the following. ☐ Set heat or air conditioning to moderate temperatures. ☐ Have lights on for evening meetings. ☐ Select a convenient, centralized location. ☐ Ensure accessibility for people with disabilities or special needs. ☐ Make sure there is more than enough (and a variety of) seating options. ☐ Prearrange for translation services (for example, someone to translate in American Sign Language [ASL]; someone to translate into the top two languages other than English). ☐ Schedule restroom and socializing breaks.
Level 1: Physiological Well-Being Tenet: Food, Shelter, Health	Assign someone to coordinate the following. ☐ Provide onsite child care with trusted staff. ☐ Have snacks or meals available. ☐ Offer transportation options. ☐ Stagger meeting times to accommodate caregivers' various work schedules. ☐ Make arrangements for inclement weather (for example, an alternative indoor location). ☐ Go to them (for example, community center, apartment complex courtyard, religious institutions). ☐ Send home appropriate takeaways or door prizes.

Source: Adapted from Maslow, 1943, 1971.

CHAPTER 6

Stage 6: Gather and Analyze Data

So *what does it all mean? What's next?* Leadership teams must carefully analyze the data collected through stakeholder engagement and the pilot phase in order to draw conclusions and get closer to a decision. Before diving directly into the data, however, you should create the following conditions for analysis in advance.

1. Predetermine monitoring and benchmarks at regular intervals to assess progress.

2. Meet regularly with your team involved in stages 2 and 3 to reflect on information gathered and make adjustments.

3. Seek help from colleagues to troubleshoot problems along the way.

4. Brief your supervisor or senior management team. The questions they ask or reactions they have help to put the initiative into perspective of the larger scheme of things in the district.

It's tempting to get tunnel vision in this stage and fall into the trap of seeking out the data that confirms a hypothesis rather than looking at it more clinically. Most educators do not possess advanced degrees in analytics or know how to use the complex tools that professional researchers regularly utilize. Nor need they. Practitioners' methods, instead, can be more rudimentary as long as we're aware that whether it be interpreting quantitative statistics from a survey or qualitative information from a focus group, there is room for bias and misapplication of the material gathered. Often, a leader selects a tool for its ease of use rather than asking him- or herself whether the tool is the right one to accumulate the desired evidence.

These goals are not mutually exclusive and, with some forethought, the chosen instrument can get straight to the root of the initiative. In his book *Surveys in Social Research*, David de Vaus (2014) explains:

> The course that a piece of research actually takes will be peculiar to that piece of research; it is affected by the research topic, the technique of data collection, the experience and personality of the researcher, the "politics" of the research, the types of people or situation being studied, funding, and so on. (p. 7)

In a sense, it's not about finding the perfect research implement, but having a keen awareness of how whichever process you choose might affect the outcomes.

This chapter offers different methods, such as surveys and focus groups, to extract the data you need and examine what it might indicate for your initiative implementation.

SURVEYS

Surveys tend to be a fan favorite in education. We survey people all the time, yet don't always know how to make sense of the evidence; or the questions asked don't result in the feedback we're looking for. A good survey involves four main components: (1) research, (2) design, (3) administration, and (4) analysis.

Research includes thinking about the purpose of the survey and determining who the target audience will be. This means figuring out the *why* behind the data collection tool—why are we doing this survey, and why is this the right group of people to ask? After those questions are answered, selecting the appropriate *design* is next. There are a multitude of options for designing survey questions, including open- or closed-ended prompts as well as deciding how many items to add. *Administering* the survey can be done online, through other digital means, or by hard copy. There are many web-based choices that guide the user through the development and delivery phases and assist with analysis. *Analyzing* the data collected is the final step in the survey process. At the end of this chapter, three reproducibles (pages 97–99) will help your team plan for a comprehensive survey process to meet your goals and intended outcomes based on the components described in the following sections.

RESEARCH

First, we have to decide on the purpose behind the survey—is it to gather a massive quantity of responses; is it to allow anonymity and elicit truths; is it to cull key words and phrases into themes? It may be all of those things and more, but defining the purpose or purposes is key. A survey should not be so broad that it results in watered-down conclusions. For example, if you are seeking feedback to find the weaknesses in an implementation, the survey should query respondents on that front. Adding other kinds of questions may distract the focus and add extraneous details, muddying up the true intention.

The second criterion is target audience. From whom do we want input? Hint: the answer is not *everyone*. The more clearly we zero in on the target, the more likely it is to hit the mark. Sometimes there will be multiple targets, thus the need for multiple surveys. Soliciting input on an initiative that touches parents, teachers, and students, such as a new high school mathematics course series to meet graduation requirements, might be done through separate survey tools.

Questions for the mathematics instructors will be more geared toward depth of content knowledge, preparation, training, and formative assessment of the course organization. Student prompts may ask about their observations, understanding of the material, and readiness. In the outer circle are parents and families, two degrees of separation from the direct experience. Since parents' or guardians' knowledge base is primarily based on their own personal background in mathematics instruction and from what they hear from their high schoolers, the questions might be designed to suss out misconceptions, gaps in understanding, and expectations. Each of the three surveys may include a question or two that are identical to look for differences and similarities across groups, but the rest should be earmarked for each particular audience.

DESIGN

Survey design is the next consideration. As referenced in the previous example related to the new mathematics requirement, figuring out *who*, *what*, and *how* to ask is critical. In this automated era of pick and click, asking too many questions, making people think too hard, or not getting straight to the point can tank a survey. Participants may drop out midway through at the slightest whim, so you have to keep them invested to the end. Length is only one factor, but an important one. Think about your own experiences with taking surveys; while different people may have various thresholds for attention span and persistence, shorter, more concise surveys may offer the best benefit for everyone.

Selecting the right wording and phrasing is more important than most people think it is and needs the proper attention. Vocabulary that is too sophisticated may cause participants to skip a question or answer it in a way that doesn't reflect their true feelings. Paying close attention to accessibility also means not just word choice but also how questions might translate into other languages in the school community. Using American slang, educational jargon, technical terms, or acronyms may confuse anyone unfamiliar with those expressions. Soliciting input on a dual immersion program, for instance, should obviously be conducted in the languages spoken by families involved. Releasing the English and translated versions at the same time also reinforces that all responses are equally valued.

Insiders often overlook the potential repercussions of accessibility, not only with the phrasing but with the visual design of the survey. Survey designers must be cognizant of making the survey usable for people with impairments, families with slow internet connections, and those who only have mobile devices available. Paper copies should also be made available to those without technology or for those who prefer that alternative.

By limiting access to participants who only speak English, possess a certain level of education or literacy skills, socioeconomic status, or ability, the results will be skewed toward those populations. If the objective is to reach the widest array of participants affected by the new initiative, we must think outside the traditional survey box. Newer survey designs sometimes include images or icons (such as happy or sad faces) in addition to or instead of text. Open-ended questions allow people to use their own words to express themselves in their own terms. Personalized surveys are also popular; the survey taker's answers to early questions customize the follow-up questions offered. The variety of options are seemingly endless.

ADMINISTRATION

Administering the survey is next. As if the design were not complicated enough, how to deliver the survey brings its own challenges. If we can make it happen, a captive audience is ideal: students in a classroom; parents or families at back-to-school night; teachers at a staff meeting; or employees at a training. If we can get the tool into their hands, we can gather the data set right then and there. This also makes for a more controlled and cleaner environment. We know who is taking the survey and how often.

On the flip side, as soon as we hit *send* on a digital survey, it's out of our control. When distributed online, through email or social media, one never knows if a single person is taking it fifty times to manipulate the outcomes in his or her favor. Furthermore, as seen in the case of online petitions, people from all over the world may weigh in on local decisions that don't affect them personally. As ubiquitous as social media is, surveys conducted in that venue can spread across a community, resulting in overwhelming and inconsistent outcomes.

We can better contain results by requiring a login or setting the survey up so that only one computer IP address is allowable per administration. Pencil-and-paper versions are an alternative, but they also have their limitations. Translating handwritten information into an electronic platform for analysis is drudgery, for one. It's also inefficient from a time investment perspective. It all depends on the scale and what we're willing to commit. Regardless, committing to sharing the results with contributors may increase their motivation to provide their opinions.

ANALYSIS

The final step in the survey process is conducting the analysis. Depending on the effort made in the first three design elements, the data mined will be of great use and service (or not so much). Also depending on the questioning technique, the data may arrive in different formats. Multiple choice and forced ranking quantitative responses can be distilled into snapshots that show straight percentages or raw numbers. We can easily capture direct *yes* or *no*, rating scales, and multiple choice responses in charts, graphs, or tables. Open-ended questions or comments paired with closed-ended options will need qualitative interpretation. There are many virtual tools using artificial intelligence available for this analysis, or we can do it manually by reading responses and sorting them into meaningful categories. Once analyzed, it's beneficial to communicate the final determinations with stakeholders, including telling them how you will use the information to improve the new initiative.

CASE STUDY

Homework Policy

Several parents of middle school students in the district have been airing frequent concerns about the amount of homework assigned. After several emails and public comments to the school board that teachers are not following the adopted homework policies, the school board directs staff to develop a survey to find out how widespread the problem might be. The assessment team creates a simple five-question survey to get at the root of the issue—is the policy itself the problem, or is the problem how teachers are applying the policy?

Figure 6.1 shows the survey, which contains closed and open-ended questions to allow the assessment department to collect both types of data.

Dear District Parents,

We have been hearing a lot of feedback recently on the district's homework policy and would like to reach out formally to gather data on how well it's working for our students. Please take a few minutes to share your thoughts and experiences with the policy itself and how it's being implemented. We will share the results with staff and the community and recommend future actions to the school board. Thank you for your participation!

1. Is your child's teacher following the current district homework policy of no more than sixty to ninety minutes total of homework per weekday?

    a. All teachers are following the time limits stated in the policy.

    b. Most teachers are following the time limits stated in the policy.

    c. A few teachers are following the time limits stated in the policy.

    d. None of the teachers are following the time limits stated in the policy.

Figure 6.1: Homework policy survey.   continued ▶

2. How much time is your child spending on average per weekday on homework?
   a. Thirty to sixty minutes
   b. Sixty to ninety minutes
   c. Ninety to one hundred twenty minutes
   d. More than one hundred twenty minutes
3. How often is your child's teacher assigning homework to complete over the weekend?
   a. Never on the weekend (per the policy)
   b. Infrequently on the weekend
   c. Some weekends
   d. Every weekend
4. What impact is the amount of homework having on your child's well-being (for example, feeling stressed and overwhelmed, affecting sleep habits, or experiencing anxiety or illness)?
   a. No noticeable impact
   b. Low impact
   c. Medium impact
   d. High impact
5. What suggestions do you have to improve the district's homework policy or teachers' application of it? (open-ended response)

After distributing the survey electronically through the parent portal in the district's student information system, and also setting up kiosks for parents to input responses during parent conference week, the district receives nearly 2,400 replies. Once the assessment team analyzes the results, staff present three conclusive findings at the next school board meeting: (1) the policy itself seems to be clearly outlined and does not need much tweaking; (2) more than half the teachers regularly assign work that goes beyond the time limits; and (3) more than 70 percent of parents report that the amount of homework is negatively affecting their child's well-being.

The board suggests a few changes in wording on the policy to enhance clarity; asks the professional learning department to design some trainings for teachers on the purpose and function of assigning homework; and requires each school site grade-level and subject-area team to develop a weekly calendar to calibrate the amount and types of homework they are handing out. After ten weeks, staff will then conduct a follow-up survey to see if the resolutions are working.

In the hypothetical homework policy survey, the leadership team demonstrates it is employing Hargie's (2011) theory for boosting stakeholders' psychological safety concerning competence, relatedness, and autonomy. When survey participants have the opportunity to share their feedback, it helps them reclaim some sense of agency regarding a topic that heavily impacts their families' lives. Furthermore, it can bolster better cooperation between teachers, students, and parents to find mutually agreeable solutions to a shared problem. Surveying can be an excellent way to garner initial responses that schools and districts can build on with additional modes, such as focus groups.

FOCUS GROUPS

Another popular mode for assembling data in educational settings is holding focus groups. Since schools are in the people industry, having face-to-face meetings with their stakeholders helps build trust and support for a new initiative. Simultaneously, they provide the opportunity to clear up misunderstandings and gain valuable firsthand perspectives.

George Kamberelis and Greg Dimitriadis (2013) state:

> Understanding focus groups and their dynamics through multiple angles of vision forces us always to see the world in new and unexpected ways. We remain less tempted by the lures of simple facticity or transcendence—pulled always to see our empirical material in new and more rigorous ways. (p. 16)

Focus groups have their own four unique ingredients to keep in mind when contemplating whether or not to employ them: (1) location, (2) moderator, (3) participants, and (4) intended results. In the action planning section at the end of this chapter, the "Focus Group Mapping Tool" reproducible (page 98) will help your team map out your particular focus group process in each of these areas.

LOCATION

The location includes physical comfort, emotional safety, and transparency (including whether or not the session will be recorded or kept confidential). As in the previous chapter, we must consider Maslow's (1943, 1971) hierarchy of needs when it comes to the focus group setting. Does it elicit feelings of security or trigger fears? Is it inviting to all, or does it exclude or alienate certain populations? Operating out of convenience, educators may choose places they're comfortable in, but others may not be. Neutrality is important. Holding a focus group for students in the main office might seem like a safe place to the adults, but the teens may associate it with being in trouble. The school library might be a better alternative gathering place. Likewise, a public setting or other community gathering space could be used for parent groups instead of a school multiuse room to lessen potential anxiety.

MODERATOR

Selecting the right moderator is essential as well. This person must be trustworthy, a good facilitator, knowledgeable about the topic, adept in strategies to bring out issues and truths, and able to balance the speakers' talking and listening time. Good moderators must be careful not to lead the discussion in any particular direction to avoid bias, but rather gently ask probing questions that get at the crux of participants' experiences. This may sound obvious, but the moderator should also be likable—someone who naturally engenders care and connection. Making the group at ease with the moderator and with each other in a short period of time takes a special talent.

PARTICIPANTS

As with the surveying method, schools and districts should meticulously select target audiences. They must consider whether to organize participants homogeneously or heterogeneously. Groups with demographically like participants may fortify certain themes that they agree or disagree on. Those that consist of more diverse individuals could draw out deeper thinking as contrasting voices challenge each other's perspectives. Both options have their merits and limitations. Regardless, since psychological welfare is essential, separating out students from staff and parents is more likely to draw out honesty and candor.

INTENDED RESULTS

The recordings or transcripts from focus group sessions will provide a host of qualitative data for analysis. The results may come in the form of narratives, quotations, videos, pictures, tones of voice, frequency of phrasing, or analysis of body language or other unspoken cues. Again, one does not have to be a professional researcher to whittle down the key bits of information compiled; however, this is not as linear a process as a quantitative study, so looking at the data from all angles is advisable.

Expanding on the brief example mentioned earlier about seeking feedback from parents of students in the language immersion program, cultural and linguistic awareness may also be a factor. The parents of White, English-speaking students in a Spanish dual immersion program likely have different background experiences and maybe even expectations or goals for their children than those from Latinx or Hispanic heritage. When analyzing participants' reactions to different prompts, it's also important to be aware of one's own assumptions or possible misinterpretations stemming from differing cultural means of expression. Colleagues who share similar backgrounds as the participants are an invaluable resource to tap when analyzing the focus group results. Even better, partnering with them throughout the whole exercise will enrich the overall process.

Let's make this more concrete by examining the following case study.

CASE STUDY

Spanish Dual Immersion Program

A school district has Spanish dual immersion programs located in four of the city's forty-five schools. For decades, parents and teachers have expressed a desire to combine all four strands into one at a currently vacant K–8 school site. They develop a task force and hold several focus group meetings to hear from the community. They use the template in figure 6.2 to make notations and reveal if there are certain patterns of responses from which they can draw conclusions.

A = Agreement (verbal or nonverbal)

D = Disagreement (verbal or nonverbal)

SE = Significant statement or example suggests agreement

SD = Significant statement or example suggests disagreement

NR = Neither agreement nor disagreement (nonresponse)

Focus Group Questions	Member 1	Member 2	Member 3	Member 4	Member 5	Member 6
1. Would your family stay in the Spanish dual immersion program if all four current programs united at a single site?	SD	A	A	D	SE	SE
2. Would transportation be an issue for your family if we relocated the program to the vacant school site?	A	D	NR	SD	SE	NR
3. If we offered different extracurricular programs at the new school, would you still be interested in enrolling?	D	SD	SD	A	A	A

Source: Adapted from Onwuegbuzie et al., 2009, p. 8.

Figure 6.2: Assessing consensus in a focus group.

The next step is drawing conclusions from the aggregate responses for each row of questions. Based on the sample in figure 6.2, it appears that four of six parents agree that they will keep their children enrolled if unifying at a single site. When it comes to transportation issues, the data is inconclusive and the leader should probe more deeply into that question. Finally, six respondents for question three on extracurriculars are divided down the middle, and perhaps the prompt should be more specific to define what those differences between schools might be.

When coming across inconsistencies or question marks in the sense-making phase of interpreting focus group data, it can be helpful to corroborate tentative findings with supplemental data from passive sources. Educators can tap into many pre-existing resources to bring a fuzzy picture into greater focus, such as those in the following section.

SUPPLEMENTAL DATA COMPILATION METHODS

There are many passive approaches to data collection and interpretation. Much can be gleaned from electronic resources, such as the frequency with which students log on to a new online program, the amount of time they spend on a task or progress through the material, and how often teachers interact with students within the platform. Attendance rates, academic transcripts, standardized assessment scores, and graduation and dropout rates may also indicate findings related to a new initiative's implementation. We must be careful not to attribute such high-level data points to a specific project alone since many variables contribute to longitudinal trends. Instead, these passive data may be used to refute or confirm the information gathered from other intentionally designed tools such as surveys, focus groups, interviews, and observations. Figure 6.3 provides samples that might be gathered as part of the data collection and analysis process for three different scenarios.

Initiative	Data Needed	Passive Source
1. Align district's mathematics pathways to reflect the Common Core State Standards	Longitudinal standardized achievement scores in mathematics	Provincial ministry or state department of education accountability data website Reports from national testing consortiums (for example, College Board, Partnership for Assessment of Readiness for College and Careers [PARCC], and Smarter Balanced Assessment Consortium [SBAC]) Database of district mathematics benchmarks and summative test results
	Analysis of existing mathematics options at all secondary schools	Download current pathways from district website. Review high school course catalogues.
	Demographics on historical enrollment in grade 7–12 mathematics courses	Run report from student information system. Review academic transcripts for course enrollment and pupil distribution.

2. Reduction and consolidation of school bus routes from thirty-five down to twenty as a cost-savings measure	Information on current transportation routes	Examine map of existing bus routes. Collect public transportation schedules and station locations.
	Bus ridership over the past five years	Review videos from bus cameras. Download sensor data for entries and exits at each bus stop. Gather accounting documents for historical bus pass sales from the transportation department.
	Number of students that qualify for free and reduced price meals (FRPM) and housing concentrations in the city	Load report from student information system. Collect participation statistics from Child Nutrition Services. Compile data from cafeteria point-of-sales devices. Assemble heat map of where students qualifying for FRPM program primarily live.
3. Evaluation of all current digital communications tools to determine which to renew and which to discontinue supporting	Quantitative data from each of the communication services	Request digital traffic reports, including number of visitors per day, popular times of day, type of data accessed, popular pages, downloaded files, and so on.
	Qualitative data from parent and staff social media comments and discussion threads	Scan social media chatter (Facebook, NextDoor, Twitter) on themes related district communications. Review board meeting minutes or notes from other public forums to compile the number of positive and negative comments.
	Costs for license renewals, tech support, and other resources	Access financial records and approved budgets on initial purchases plus any renewals. Note overlaps and gaps by doing a side-by-side comparison of each tool's features as outlined in their proposals.

Figure 6.3: Data needs and passive sources.

In each of the three examples in figure 6.3, there is a plethora of already-existing resources to draw from to corroborate other active data collection efforts. Although the term *passive* is widely used to describe these types of data, our interaction with them is far from its usual connotation. The data may be readily available, but without our meticulous interpretation and judicious application to the novel situation, it will not be useful on its own.

Furthermore, making the results comprehensible and digestible for the decision makers in stage 7 is imperative. The results should be communicated clearly, confidently, and conclusively. It's important to be transparent about the unknowns and what kinds of checks and balances will be in place to counteract difficulties ahead. By this time, the leader and the initiative are closely intertwined, so having a trusted colleague review the data presentation with fresh eyes is helpful.

If the data show weak audience reception or lack of concrete quantitative impact, it may be that the difficult decision to set the initiative aside must be made. Or the researcher might want to employ different tools to see if there are contrasting results. Once strongly supported by the numbers and narratives, it's time to move it forward.

CONCLUSION

Data collection and interpretation can be administered through the relatively simple means described in this chapter or by using more sophisticated software or evaluation tools in partnership with a higher education institution or company that specializes in measurement and metrics. Using outside resources can help neutralize bias and provide expertise that a district may not have access to onsite. However, it also could mean a longer timeframe and financial impacts that the home-grown methods don't usually incur to the same degree. Regardless of the chosen options, no initiative is flawless or foolproof. But putting in the due diligence on the first six stages sets up an initiative for success in the most critical next stage of the process—decision making.

STAGE 6 ACTION PLAN: CHECKLIST AND REPRODUCIBLES

The following checklist and reproducibles help you apply what you learned in this chapter and move forward to the next stage of the initiative implementation process.

- ☐ Review components for survey design and focus groups, and then design your own using the "Survey Mapping Tool" and "Focus Group Mapping Tool" reproducibles (pages 97–98).
- ☐ Determine which passive data sources may supplement your research goals (see figure 6.3, page 94).
- ☐ Complete the "Data Analysis Form" planning template (page 99).

Survey Mapping Tool

Directions: Applying the information discussed in chapter 6, use this template as a mapping tool to plan out the key elements of your survey.

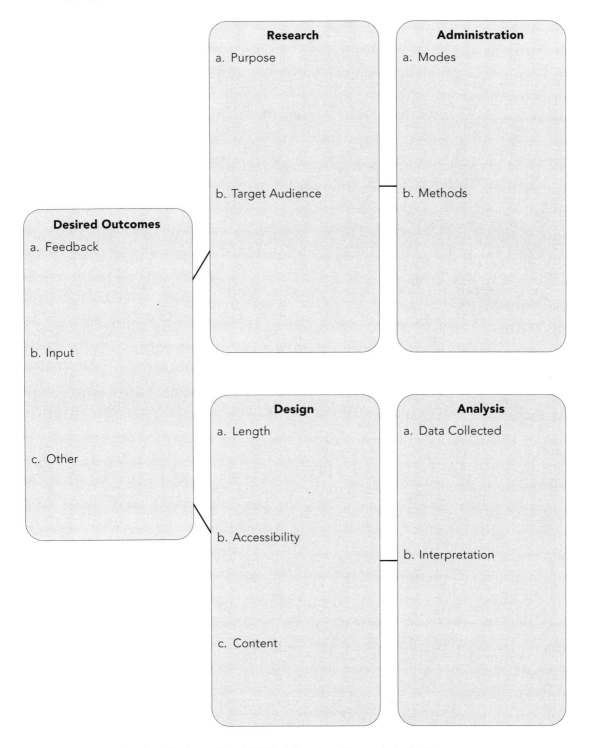

Desired Outcomes

a. Feedback

b. Input

c. Other

Research

a. Purpose

b. Target Audience

Administration

a. Modes

b. Methods

Design

a. Length

b. Accessibility

c. Content

Analysis

a. Data Collected

b. Interpretation

Focus Group Mapping Tool

Directions: Applying the information in chapter 6, use this template as a mapping tool to plan out the key elements prior to your upcoming focus group.

Desired Outcomes

a. Feedback

b. Input

c. Other

Participants

a. Demographics

b. Groupings

c. Size

Location

a. Way-Finding (for example, signage, maps, guides)

b. Neutral Environment

Moderator

a. Knowledge

b. Skills

c. Characteristics

Intended Results

a. Qualitative Data

b. Interpretation

Data Analysis Form

Directions: Regardless of the collection tools you decide to employ, this data analysis form will help guide your team's planning through the interpretation of information collected. The first row is completed with sample details from a district determining whether to conduct instruction in person, hybrid, or fully online for the following school year. The remaining rows are blank to input your own distinct endeavors.

Initiative	Desired Input	Metrics	Collection Procedure	Sample Size	Results	Interpretation
Distance and Digital Instructional Delivery Model	Input from parents and students on in-person, hybrid, or distance learning instruction	Less than 50 percent of survey respondents in agreement	Google Forms Hard copy surveys sent via email	8,950	25 percent in-person; 43 percent hybrid; 32 percent fully online	75 percent want hybrid or online only; create options for both; no in-person at this time

CHAPTER 7

Stage 7: Make a Decision

The initiative is finally ready, and it's time to make a decision. The decision isn't the leader's to make alone, however. He or she will submit a written recommendation and make a presentation to a wider team similar to that in stage 2 (pitch the proposal) and stage 3 (determine priorities). However, instead of being theoretical, this report will contain factual, reality-based results from the pilot and data analysis stages. Furthermore, it will supply more detailed and accurate estimations about costs for full implementation and the comprehensive roll-out plan.

This chapter details the ways in which the leader plans for his or her initiative's debut as a viable implementation in the district and how the leadership team comes to a conclusion on the initiative's ultimate fate.

GREEN LIGHT, YELLOW LIGHT, OR RED LIGHT

As with the first presentation conducted by the team leader in stage 2, people from all corners of the district should be represented on a newly comprised evaluation panel: human resources, business services, instructional services, employee association leaders, teachers, principals, and support staff. At this evaluation session, the team will come to consensus on whether the initiative is ready for launch based on the work done to date in the first six stages as well as the current status of the project. The "Questions and Commitments Notetaking Tool" reproducible (page 110) at the end of this chapter will assist the team in determining whether to green-light, yellow-light, or red-light the initiative.

GREEN-LIGHT THE INITIATIVE (MOVE FROM PILOT TO IMPLEMENTATION)

Green-lighting is the ideal outcome, but not easily attained. When a team green-lights a project, it means that it has at least 90 percent of the ingredients needed to be approved for implementation. Resources have been secured and are intact for the duration. This particular program is ready to be prioritized above other district initiatives. Kinks have been worked out through the piloting phase. Data show positive results for students. The plan has moral and operational support from key stakeholders in the school or district. Communications and professional development have been widely disbursed and favorably reviewed. The boxes are all checked, and the team feels confident that it will be a success. Following are the stages 1 through 6 criteria for green-lighting an initiative.

- Excellent research and planning
- Strong proposal
- High prioritization
- Successful pilot
- Positive engagement feedback
- Supportive data

YELLOW-LIGHT THE INITIATIVE (EXTEND THE PROTOTYPE PHASE OR ASK FOR MORE DATA)

Yellow-lighting is a more common outcome when a plan gets presented. It has the moral support to move forward but needs a few more concrete pieces in place to do so. It may be that the funding source hasn't yet been identified or that the professional development is taking longer than originally anticipated. When coming to a yellow light, we might need to slow down or yield to another initiative in line before it. During this period of pausing, the leader will bolster the project by filling in the gaps outlined by the team during the group discussion that follows. Following are the stages 1 through 6 criteria for yellow-lighting an initiative.

- Sufficient research and planning
- Adequate proposal
- Medium prioritization
- Satisfactory pilot
- Mixed engagement feedback
- Inconclusive data

RED-LIGHT THE INITIATIVE (HALT IMPLEMENTATION OR REQUIRE SIGNIFICANT CHANGES AND RETURN TO EARLIER STAGE)

It is rather rare to have the initiative fully red-lighted this far into the process. There are typically red flags along the way to suggest that it's not going well. In looking at the data, the benefits to student learning just aren't there, or there is a lackluster response or negative reaction from a particular stakeholder group. Sometimes things are going well, and then external conditions suddenly arise that stop the idea from proceeding. Employees go on strike. The bottom drops out of the economy, sparking a major recession. Legislation changes. A worldwide pandemic hits that closes school for the remainder of the school year. Both internal and external factors can turn an otherwise yellow-lighted initiative into red. But in either case, it was likely never going to make the cut. Following are the stages 1 through 6 criteria for red-lighting an initiative.

- Insufficient research and planning
- Weak proposal
- Low prioritization
- Unsatisfactory pilot
- Negative engagement feedback
- Unsupportive data

See page 114 or visit **go.SolutionTree.com/leadership** for a free reproducible showing all the criteria for green-lighting, yellow-lighting, and red-lighting a project.

In their work on group decision making, Thomas Saaty and Kirti Peniwati (2013) elaborate that:

> This process requires the participation of every member. Often a group task calls for the application of expertise beyond that of a single person. Individual competence is necessary but not sufficient because accomplishing a group task is not simply a matter of coming up with a decision. The group also needs to work on enhancing its cohesiveness because the quality of its decisions depends on the ability of its members to function collectively as a coherent unit. The group decision-making process needs to bring satisfaction to its members by achieving the task and creating desire to participate in future sessions. In a way, each group session is an investment in developing a long-term collaborative climate. (p. 16)

This sought-after sense of interdependence is one that begins to permeate the institution the more frequently teams apply the stages of the new initiative protocol to future implementations.

CASE STUDY

Graduation Requirements

A director of secondary education takes her assembled team through an initiative to institute an e-learning course as part of the district's high school graduation requirements. Students who go on to higher education and most workforce settings will be expected to take online classes toward their degree or virtual seminars for professional development. The purpose of the requirement is to prepare K–12 students for postsecondary life with a supportive experience in an online learning environment prior to leaving the system. Many states and school districts already have such programs in place, so although new to this district, various models have been established elsewhere.

The team listens to the presentation and fills out a chart with their questions and ways that they personally pledge to support the plan. See figure 7.1.

Participant	Questions	Support or Commitments
Certificated Human Resources Director	What kind of professional development (PD) will be offered? Is there special credentialing needed to teach online courses?	My department will help with the licensing aspects to make sure we're in compliance with the state. I will contact some technology-savvy teachers who might be interested in leading professional development.
Chief Technology Officer	Are you planning to provide devices for students without them to ensure access and equity? What about internet service for low-income families? How will we create privacy safeguards and firewalls when the students are logging on at home?	We will have to look into increasing our bandwidth to ensure high-speed connectivity. I think there may be some special grant funding available we can take advantage of to support low-income students. I wonder how we might attach this to our upcoming Google Apps for Education launch.
Teachers' Association President	Will you be taking volunteers or requiring all high school teachers to deliver online instruction? What kind of compensation will be provided for training?	We will need to renegotiate the teaching conditions section of the collective bargaining agreement (CBA) to outline mutual expectations. Let's collaborate on a joint memorandum of understanding (MOU) to distribute to employees explaining the new initiative.

Special Education Director	Do you have examples from other districts for students with special needs? What Universal Design for Learning (UDL) strategies can be embedded in the online classroom management system? How can we leverage paraeducators for support?	We need to consider new accommodations if we require all students with Individualized Education Plans (IEPs) to participate. Our program specialists and school psychologists will create presentations for general education teachers with best online practices for students with disabilities.
High School Principal	Will this be required for incoming ninth graders at all high schools this fall, or are we going to phase it in more slowly? Can we get two extra PD days built into the schedule to help teachers get ready?	I will work with the other principals to make sure we're all in alignment so the requirement is communicated and applied fairly across the district. We can also help with writing the course description so it gets approved by the university system for credit.
PTA President	Are there any particular skills that parents need to know in order to help their children with learning via this new curriculum? How is the district going to communicate with parents about why there will be a change in graduation requirements?	At the next districtwide PTA meeting, I will save time for you to present the plan for our leadership so they can communicate our support clearly at the site level. We would be happy to work with local businesses to get input from them on the skills they would like to see in our graduates so it can be included in the new course.
Student Representative to the Board of Education	Will this prevent anyone from graduating if they can't complete the class? What will be done to prevent academic dishonesty, which we know is a big problem with students already?	Having participated in the pilot at our high school, I can help out with sharing the student experience with the teachers. Maybe we can organize a donation drive to raise funds to purchase Chromebooks for students without devices.
Attendance Clerk	Can we use our current student information system (SIS) to track attendance? How will we know if someone is absent?	Once we're trained, our lead clerks will develop a step-by-step video to show others how to take attendance for virtual classes.

Figure 7.1: Questions and commitments notetaking tool.   continued ▶

Participant	Questions	Support or Commitments
Curriculum and Assessment Department Instructional Coach	Will the coaches be creating district-level assessments for the courses, or will they be site or teacher developed? When will our team get some training on the tools in advance of the rollout?	I love the idea to make how-to and tips and tricks videos for both teachers and students. I'm on it! We need to know how the new platform integrates with our current grading program. Teachers will not be happy if they have to use two systems. I'll email our reps and find out.

After the leader answers questions posed by the team and has committed momentum for moving forward, the project is heading down the road to green-lighting. However, after further discussion, there are still several pieces to put into place prior to a full-scale launch, so the team downgrades it to yellow status. The supply of available devices must be inventoried and other technical details worked out, such as internet access for all families. A robust and differentiated professional development system also must be formulated for teachers. Getting the new requirement approved by the state university system and communicating to staff and families warrants a longer runway as well.

Since it is already March, the team consults the prioritization rubric from stage 3 (see figure 3.2, page 39) and recalibrates the placement of the new initiative. Team members collectively decide to start the requirement for second-semester tenth graders the following school year, since the students will already have a fair amount of the high school experience behind them. It also will give them ample time between then and their senior year to retake the course if not successful the first time around.

As an interim step, they realize that the e-learning initiative dovetails with another one that has been waiting in the wings. After a year of piloting, the district recently green-lighted adopting Google Apps for Education (GAFE) for students and staff. Part of this team as well, the director of instructional technology shares the memo he had planned to send to parents explaining how the platform will be implemented that coming fall. The leadership team also presented to the school board that spring so they could be briefed on the elements and determine if the pending project was being properly prepared for implementation.

Since the GAFE project will be able to support the new graduation requirement, the leadership team suggests adding a preview to connect the two, as shown in the parent letter in figure 7.2.

Dear Parents and Guardians:

After a year of piloting the program on a smaller scale and as part of the district's mission to become a leading center of educational innovation and support our goal of using technology to expand learning opportunities for students, we are proud to partner with Google Apps for Education (GAFE/Google Apps) starting in August. GAFE is used by thousands of K–12 districts and universities worldwide and comes with a set of online tools for communication, collaboration, time management, and document storage.

Provided by Google to the district at no cost, these tools are housed on the internet, and you can access them from any internet-connected computer with a web browser.

- **Mail:** Email account for school use managed by the district
- **Calendar:** Calendar offering users the ability to organize schedules, daily activities, and assignments
- **Docs:** Word processing, spreadsheet, drawing, and presentation toolset similar to Microsoft Office
- **Sites:** Individual and collaborative website creation tool
- **Drive:** File storage for documents

Google Apps make it possible for students to work together virtually on documents, presentations, and projects via the internet. Google Apps eliminates most needs for flash drives by allowing students to share files and electronically submit assignments to their teachers. Email accounts allow teachers and students to communicate and collaborate in a safe and structured way. Web-based learning tools provide free access to storytelling, concept mapping, video editing, and visual presentation tools.

The district will be purchasing several Chromebooks for instructional and assessment uses, whose features are greatly enhanced by access to Google Apps.

The district technology advisory committee (DTAC) also recommends supplying Google Apps for Education tools to students and staff for the following reasons.

- Give students practice in using current technology applications and tools.
- Give students the ability to work on assignments and documents using common, no-cost tools both at school and at home.
- Facilitate paperless transfer of work between students and teachers.
- Provide adequate, long-term storage space for student work.
- Help students work collaboratively, engage in peer-editing of documents, and publish for a wider audience.
- Prepare students for college and career readiness, including a possible future graduation requirement for them to take an online course in their tenth-grade year.
- In order to ensure student safety, students will only be able to email and share documents with their teachers and other students within the district. Google Apps for Education is equipped with a robust software program that gives the district control over applications and content, restricts access to non-approved applications or content, and allows administrators to establish policies specifying who their users can interact with. District staff will monitor student accounts to ensure compliance with the district's Student Responsible Use of Technology Agreement.

Teachers will be offered professional development training on best practices for Google Apps for instruction, and parents and students will receive information about the implementation of GAFE in the fall. We look forward to your feedback and participation!

Figure 7.2: Parent letter for Google Apps for Education implementation.

The leader polls the team for its personal level of fidelity to the initiative. There must be a certain level of trust and honesty between the key players; false or insincere lip service for support is worse than having the initiative red-lighted. Each person in the room states what he or she can and will do as action steps within the next six months to ensure a healthy launch. After being briefed, the superintendent and senior cabinet direct the leader to create a presentation for the school board meeting in April as a fully endorsed district initiative. This is the final stamp of approval needed to begin systematizing the implementation. It is also the first of many opportunities for the community to hear about the addition of e-learning as a graduation requirement. If the school board notes any concerns, the team will have time to work through the issues and smooth the pathway for the January kickoff.

This case study illustrates how many different paths can lead to the desired destination. Collaborative decision making widens perspectives on how one new initiative can link to others in the system and strengthen the whole organization as a result. While some of the earlier stages are more myopic by nature, in stage 7, we use a wider-angle lens to incorporate both preexisting approaches, current realities, and future aspirations simultaneously. Often, a *zeitgeist* of sorts descends upon the team, providing a sixth sense that an initiative is ripe and ready (or not).

THE ART AND SCIENCE OF DECISION MAKING

The decision-making stage is not always as streamlined as in the previous scenario, however, and yellow- and red-lighting happen rather frequently. Usually a project that's red-lighted has had warning signs all along and has limped along to the finish line of stage 7—if it even gets there at all. These sorts of initiatives usually have one or two champions that really believe in them, even if the rest of the school or district isn't in sync. This doesn't mean they are bad initiatives, per se, but they may be ill-timed or ill-matched to the needs of the school community. Resurfacing at a different point or reconfiguring may help, but a red-lighted initiative is considered terminated for anytime in the near future.

Remember that the whole purpose of the new initiative protocol is to allow only the fittest to survive. There is as much art as science to launching a new initiative. While your team already has many practical tools at its disposal, it's also important to recognize that not everything that matters can be measured, predicted, or planned for. We cannot discount the human element; people at the center of the implementation may not behave or respond in clinically expected ways. Taking their reactions into consideration and pivoting when necessary is the art of leadership. Thus the decision-making stage is pivotal; once green-lighted, the district has staked its resources, committed its efforts, and shifted its attention to making it thrive. All hands are on deck. Other projects may need to be put aside. This is part of the district's new identity. They have pledged to support it and see it thrive.

CONCLUSION

Stage 7 is the most pivotal phase in the process for a new initiative. The preceding six stages have finally led to fruition. The relief that comes with a decision to move forward is palpable. The leadership team has put in enormous time and effort to get the implementation ready for launch. Along with that sense of relief, there is also usually tangible enthusiasm and excitement surrounding the initiative. Then the hard work set in. The final three stages in the process described in the following chapters are designed to harness the district's energy toward this and other related programs already in place. The goal is to create synchronicity and alignment through professional development, adopt the new program or service into the fold, and provide ongoing, long-term support. Chapter 8 (page 115) starts off with instilling the importance of quality professional development and ongoing learning opportunities to cement the new initiative in place for the long haul.

STAGE 7 ACTION PLAN: CHECKLIST AND REPRODUCIBLES

The following checklist and reproducibles help you apply what you learned in this chapter and move forward to the next stage of the initiative implementation process.

- ☐ During the leader's presentation, use the "Questions and Commitments Notetaking Tool" reproducible (page 110) to note any questions or concerns. See the completed sample in figure 7.1 (page 104).

- ☐ After the presentation, have each team member complete the "Decision-Making Rubric" and "Team Decision-Making Assessment" reproducibles (pages 111–112).

- ☐ Review the criteria on the "Criteria for Green-Lighting, Yellow-Lighting, or Red-Lighting an Initiative" reproducible (page 114), and craft specific definitions to your own initiative.

Questions and Commitments Notetaking Tool

Directions: As you listen to the team leader's presentation, complete the following chart with your questions and ways that you will personally pledge to support implementation of the new initiative.

Participant	Questions	Support or Commitments

Leading the Launch © 2022 Solution Tree Press • SolutionTree.com
Visit **go.SolutionTree.com/leadership** to download this page.

Decision-Making Rubric

Directions: Evaluate the initiative against the work conducted in stages 1–6 of the initiative implementation process. Before marking the boxes, discuss with your team what metrics or markers constitute whether each stage has been successfully executed or not.

Stage 1–6 Criteria	Red	Yellow	Green
1. Research and Planning	Insufficient	Sufficient	Excellent
2. Proposal	Weak	Adequate	Strong
3. Prioritization	Low	Medium	High
4. Pilot	Unsatisfactory	Satisfactory	Successful
5. Engagement Feedback	Negative	Mixed	Positive
6. Data Analysis	Unsupportive	Inconclusive or mixed	Supportive

Team Decision-Making Assessment

Directions: Each team member can use this decision-making rubric to assess whether an initiative will move forward or not. Rate each item on a scale of 1–5, 1 being the least effective and 5 being the most effective. Then put a checkmark next to the recommendation you agree with.

Team Assessment of the Decision-Making Process	Rating Scale 1–5
Team objectives in the decision-making process were clear from the start.	1 2 3 4 5
Information was sought from a variety of people and sources.	1 2 3 4 5
Issues were framed in ways that encouraged the exploration of multiple solutions.	1 2 3 4 5
Minority and dissenting viewpoints were considered in the team discussion.	1 2 3 4 5
Reliable data and statistics were used to support rationale.	1 2 3 4 5
It is evident that the proposed initiative will improve policy, progress, or practices in the district.	1 2 3 4 5
The leader facilitated open and constructive dialogue.	1 2 3 4 5
The leader asked open-ended questions to promote understanding.	1 2 3 4 5
Everyone in the group participated equitably.	1 2 3 4 5
Team members listened attentively to the viewpoints of others.	1 2 3 4 5
Team members participated as unbiased critical thinkers rather than advocates of particular interests.	1 2 3 4 5
Team members took time to ask questions and debate options before coming to agreement.	1 2 3 4 5
Total Points: 45–60 Highly Effective 30–44 Moderately Effective 12–20 Ineffective	

Leading the Launch © 2022 Solution Tree Press • SolutionTree.com
Visit **go.SolutionTree.com/leadership** to download this page.

Individual Team Member Recommendation
Perfect: It's truly the best choice and cannot be improved upon.
Consensus: I agree and will support without reservation.
Informed Consent: The details may not be perfect, but it is close enough for me to support it here and outside the meeting as well.
Reservations: I have reservations and would like more discussion. I may then move up to consensus or consent, move down to concern, or agree with the group decision. I will not second-guess the decision outside this meeting.
Concerns: I have fundamental concerns, so I am not able to support this initiative at this time.
Disagreement: I do not agree; this is in conflict with my values, beliefs, and professional experience.

Final Recommendation	
	☐ Red-light the project
	☐ Yellow-light the project
	☐ Green-light the project

Criteria for Green-Lighting, Yellow-Lighting, or Red-Lighting an Initiative

Following are stages 1 through 6 criteria for green-lighting, yellow-lighting, or red-lighting an initiative.

Green-Lighting Criteria
Excellent research and planning
Strong proposal
High prioritization
Successful pilot
Positive engagement feedback
Supportive data
Yellow-Lighting Criteria
Sufficient research and planning
Adequate proposal
Medium prioritization
Satisfactory pilot
Mixed engagement feedback
Inconclusive data
Red-Lighting Criteria
Insufficient research and planning
Weak proposal
Low prioritization
Unsatisfactory pilot
Negative engagement feedback
Unsupportive data

CHAPTER 8

Stage 8: Plan and Deliver Professional Development

Professional development is the linchpin for any successful measure. It can and will absolutely make or break an implementation. The true believers that have developed and stand fiercely behind the new program, process, or service must recognize that the end users are not in the same place. *Yet*. Though it's sometimes the *how* that gets in the way of their embracing new practices, especially if technology is involved or there are other technical skills to be acquired, it's usually the *why* that gets lost in the shuffle. An essential element of professional development, no matter how it's delivered, is to first root the audience in the meaning and purpose behind the initiative.

This chapter will correlate Linda Darling-Hammond, Maria Hyler, and Madelyn Gardner's (2017) findings on teacher professional development design elements, as well as Willard Daggett's (2015) watershed work on rigor, relevance, and relationships designed for student engagement, and apply them to instructing adult learners.

KEY FEATURES OF EFFECTIVE PROFESSIONAL DEVELOPMENT

Darling-Hammond and colleagues (2017) identify seven widely shared features for designing professional development for teachers. Specifically, they found that effective professional development includes the following characteristics:

1. Is content focused
2. Incorporates active learning utilizing adult learning theory
3. Supports collaboration, typically in job-embedded contexts
4. Uses models and modeling of effective practice

5. Provides coaching and expert support
6. Offers opportunities for feedback and reflection
7. Is of sustained duration (Hammond et al., 2017, p. 4)

Each of these characteristics contributes to meeting the needs of educators in a comprehensive format that expands beyond the four walls of the training facility. While professional development is typically thought of as a session, workshop, or presentation, much of the real work takes place after the initial delivery. Furthermore, Darling-Hammond and colleagues (2107) warn:

> Even the best designed PD may fail to produce desired outcomes if it is poorly implemented due to barriers such as inadequate resources, including needed curriculum materials; lack of shared vision about what high-quality instruction entails; lack of time for planning and implementing new instructional approaches; conflicting requirements, such as scripted curriculum or pacing guides; and lack of adequate foundational knowledge on the part of teachers. (p. 24)

We must be cognizant of both the best *and* worst practices to combat people's possible past experiences with insufficient planning, delivery, or learning outcomes.

A comprehensive professional development plan ensures that all involved are appropriately trained or informed about how to carry out the initiative. As Mike Schmoker (2004) famously said, "Clarity precedes competence" (p. 85). Good communication fosters that clarity. You should start by issuing a variety of communications, including an introductory memo, adding an FAQs page to the district's website, and posting a short video to explain the initiative to those involved or affected. The core team members can serve as excellent evangelists in their circles of influence to create a ripple effect throughout the school or district. A positive buzz before anyone even steps in the room for a training has an immense impact on the attitude of the participants, as they will often be more receptive to the unfamiliar learning coming their way.

While there is no magic formula, there are certain hallmarks of vibrant professional development. Daggett (2015) created a rigor and relevance framework for K–12 teacher lesson planning that we can also apply to planning effective adult learning experiences. He subsequently added a relationships framework. This work aligns well with Darling-Hammond and colleagues' (2017) seven key features of quality professional development.

Table 8.1 shows the cross-connection of concepts developed by Daggett (2015) and Darling-Hammond and colleagues (2017).

Table 8.1 Research Base for Professional Development

Daggett (2015)	Darling-Hammond and Colleagues (2017)
Rigor: The appropriate level of difficulty and challenge that prompts a participant to think, perform, and grow to new levels	Uses content-driven material Is provided with appropriate duration and frequency
Relevance: The ability for a participant to connect his or her own work or life experiences to the material being taught	Incorporates active learning utilizing adult learning theory Applies to job-embedded contexts Uses models and demonstrations of effective practice
Relationships: Connections between colleagues that enhance morale, escalate work engagement, and increase job satisfaction	Supports peer collaboration Provides coaching and expert support Offers opportunities for authentic feedback and reflection

On the surface, adult learners can be rather indistinguishable from younger ones in that they want to be appropriately challenged, draw personal associations to the material, and connect with their peers. Where the generations diverge is related to cumulative life experience, extensiveness of knowledge base, and professional learning goals or intentions. While elementary and secondary students bring with them schema and personal history as well, adults have different ambitions for learning. Many are already well-versed in the curriculum, standards, and lesson planning; some are bona fide experts in the education field. Housel (2020) explains:

> [Adult learners] are also more proactive and accustomed to making their own decisions. As more self-directed learners, adults thrive with project-based or inquiry activities where they can determine the pace and style of their own learning and incorporate "multiple intelligences" (Gardner, 1983) in the process. Consequently, instruction should be more student-centered and driven with instructors acting as guides and facilitators. (pp. 7–8)

Therefore, when applying the rigor, relevance, relationships framework (Daggett, 2015; Darling-Hammond et al., 2017) to your professional development plan, consider how to best prime the design to best support the teachers, administrators, or support staff's diverse and unique learning needs.

RIGOR

Rigor refers to content at the appropriate skill and knowledge level for participants that will extend understanding or skills beyond their current state. The material should focus on exactly what the predetermined objectives are via an adaptation of PLC critical question 1: "What do we want staff to know and be able to do?" (DuFour et al., 2016). Administering a quick pretest or self-assessment before even designing the curriculum is a good way to determine what to include in the subject matter. When there is a higher or lower level of competency or familiarity already, the presenter can spend more or less time on the basics and adjust accordingly.

Alternatively, a facilitator might realize the need to divide the instruction into multiple sessions. It may be necessary, just as in the classroom, to differentiate instruction or offer tiered trainings. Too easy and people get bored. Too hard and they get frustrated. Checking for understanding at certain points throughout the workshop and reorganizing participants into different ability groupings based on their attainment of the material will help sustain engagement.

The duration, timing, and frequency of the professional development are key elements for consideration as well. Depending on the difficulty of the topic and how cognitively demanding it might be, breaking it down into several shorter sessions with time for practical application in between can embed the learning more deeply. We often expect adults to have a longer attention span than children and, while there is no true scientific consensus on the topic, breaking down tasks and learning activities into digestible chunks is a solid strategy for maintaining participants' focus. The instructor should not only design the lesson with the appropriate amount of rigor, but he or she also should pay careful attention to the audience to gauge continued engagement. When side conversations start to pick up or people begin scrolling through their phones, it's a sign to shift gears.

RELEVANCE

While Daggett (2015) starts with rigor, I contend that the first ingredient in designing a strong professional development program is making sure that it's relevant to the audience. Not much is worse for a professional than wondering why he or she is in a room for an entire day learning about something that doesn't have anything to do with his or her job. Conversely, being left out of a training that could assist with one's development in a certain area is likewise negligent. For example, a leader might send out invitations to all elementary teachers to introduce them to a new reading program but neglect to include special education teachers and paraeducators who also work intensively with children on those same skill sets. Allowing self-selection in signing up for a workshop is one strategy to hit the relevancy target.

However, relevancy can be in the eye of the beholder. Sometimes people think that something does or doesn't apply to them based on personal perception. They may sense that the implementation is optional and unconnected from their position because they are unclear about what will be covered or have perhaps heard things about the training that aren't true. Communicating the description, objectives, and expectations for training sessions is critical. If it's mandatory, say so. If it's geared toward certain employees and not others, state that outright.

After the participants are in their seats, use models and demonstrations of effective operations applicable to job-specific contexts to connect the dots. Videos, case studies, hypothetical scenarios, role playing, Socratic seminars, and other interactive tools geared toward adult learning honors their existing expertise while expanding their thinking. Laura Desimone and Michael Garet (2015) found that active learning, such as opportunities for teachers to observe, solicit feedback, analyze student work samples, or develop lessons or presentations, rather than passive reception of the material translates to increased levels of investment and adoption of new thinking and practices. Desimone and Garet (2015) state:

> We should consider carefully the ease with which the PD can be integrated into teacher lessons. We ought to take on the issue of alignment with lessons more deliberately, and include support, guidance, and practice for teachers to integrate the knowledge or pedagogy into their daily instruction, rather than leaving that burden to them when they return to the classroom. (p. 256)

The adage that the smartest person in the room is the room is apt here as well—whole-group discussions, small-group interactions, problem-solving activities, and other instructional tasks often spur relevant, collaborative learning that enriches everyone in the environment, including the leader. Once past the relevancy hurdle, the leader must weigh what the proper amount of rigor should be.

RELATIONSHIPS

This is where relationships come in. An outside trainer may have a larger hill to climb in establishing connections with the participants in short order. But insiders, such as district or site administrators, may have other challenges due to preexisting associations or encounters with colleagues that may have been negative or unpleasant in the past. Many different techniques can be used by the trainer, as long as they are perceived as authentic. Learning and using people's names and drawing them out through storytelling or self-revelation is often effective. Having a good sense of humor and upbeat style also elicits comfort. When trainers express vulnerability, compassion, and caring, they bring down the psychological walls in the room. By creating an atmosphere of "it's OK to fail," "we're all learners here," and "progress not perfection," you provide more opportunities for participants to try something new.

Checking in and asking for feedback throughout the presentation and then making adjustments based on participant input reinforces relationship building too. The trainer should also afford ample opportunities for peer collaboration and assistance. In the times between instructional sessions, people in job-alike positions might be encouraged to contact each other for trouble-shooting and tips and tricks. If they cannot help each other, the leadership team should arrange for access to coaches or experts on a just-in-time basis. Staff cannot be expected to shelve their questions for a month or longer while waiting for the next workshop; otherwise, they will more likely shelve the whole enterprise. The go-to people at the district and site levels should always be ready to respond to knowledge or skill gaps and support those in the field.

AGENDA DESIGN

There are a multitude of interactive possibilities when designing an agenda for professional development. The goal is being intentional about how to capture the audience's attention so they walk away with the necessary knowledge and skills to implement the initiative. When designing a professional learning experience, we should keep in mind the three Rs of relevance, rigor, and relationships and where we can embed them intentionally in a workshop's activities.

Figure 8.1 shows a sample workshop agenda showing placements of the three Rs in italics. The "Professional Development Design Worksheet" reproducible (page 125) is included at the end of this chapter for your own design.

Topic	Process	Time
Prior knowledge check	Online self-assessment (*rigor*)	Five minutes
Welcome and introductions	Table talk (*relationships*)	Eight minutes
Results from self-assessment	Review data (*relevance*)	Five minutes
Content delivery	Presentation (*rigor*)	Twelve minutes
Content discussion	Jigsaw groups (*rigor*)	Twenty minutes
Job-embedded connections	Action planning (*relevance*)	Twenty minutes
Workshop feedback and next steps	Reflection (*relationships*)	Ten minutes

Figure 8.1: Sample workshop agenda.

PROFESSIONAL DEVELOPMENT SUSTAINED DELIVERY

Beyond the single workshop agenda, it's advantageous to map out an entire year or semester's worth of professional development with the flexibility to pivot as unexpected events unfold or new needs arise. Perhaps a district is implementing a new initiative to build leadership skills and growth mindsets in their current administrators. The objectives are to shift their focus from being site or department managers and supervisors to becoming visionary, mission-driven leaders that foster culturally responsive practices and increase equity throughout the school or district.

The superintendent sets up a monthly collaboration team schedule with all district office directors to sharpen and expand their own proficiencies and knowledge to then serve as role models for others, who will receive similar training in phase two of the implementation. The first forty-five minutes of each session focuses on culturally responsive leadership instruction, and the second forty-five minutes include collaboration time for planning practical application and strategies to devise action steps within each leader's specific work setting.

Figure 8.2 (page 122) outlines the first six months of lessons and assignments for the district office directors.

I cannot emphasize enough that the professional development plan the leader puts together has to be interactive, useful, and responsive to staff members' needs. Conventional wisdom demonstrates that unless the instruction is on a simple concept or skill, which can be handled in a one-time workshop, it takes time to incorporate new habits into one's daily work. Staggering the trainings gives people an opportunity to try out the tools or approaches and come back with authentic, experiential questions that when answered, will ingrain their learning more deeply. Good professional learning in advance of implementing the initiative will set up the initiative for far greater success.

CONCLUSION

Research on professional development and learning confirms the premise that single session trainings rarely improve educators' ability to incorporate new practices or significantly transform their mindsets for the long term. A study out of Alberta, Canada's Ministry of Education (as cited in InPraxis Group, 2006) posits:

> A traditional view of professional development as a single, uncontextualized event is incompatible with the complexity of professional development. Multiple environments for professional learning—different organizational structures and priorities, alternate methods for collaboration and communication in professional development approaches, and aligning professional development with elements such as district policy and curriculum needs, stress the importance of considering professional development through multiple lenses. (p. 24)

Timeline	Culturally Responsive Leadership Group Lessons	Practical Application Planning Time
August	Definition of ourselves and our district: • Develop norms, practices, and expectations. • Review board and district mission and vision, department goals, guiding principles, and values. • Review district self-evaluation results. • Present on work to date on gender spectrum, religious diversity, and anti-racism efforts.	1. Meet with your staff to share information about the new initiative and what they can expect going forward. 2. Revise your department's mission, vision, and goals to ensure inclusive language. 3. Review all documents and the department website to eliminate bias or discriminatory practices for protected groups. 4. Read the leadership versus management article prior to the next meeting.
September	Leadership and management: • Watch video clip, "The First Follower." • Discuss culturally responsive leadership versus traditional management article. • Take working styles questionnaire; conduct group discussion on how your style may increase or decrease equity for others. • Pair-share on personal strengths and growth areas.	1. Share three key ahas you had from the session with your staff about developing your own cultural competencies. 2. Have your staff take the working styles questionnaire and discuss collective results related to how your department currently functions. 3. Identify gaps and opportunities for building equitable practices into your department's daily operations. 4. Make a department commitment to increasing awareness and confronting exclusionary practices.
October	Inclusive customer service: • Watch video, "Johnny the Bagger." • Discuss how inclusion benefits the district. • Partner role play using inclusive language and active listening. • Review framework for culturally responsive leadership.	1. At your next staff meeting, show "Johnny the Bagger" video and brainstorm ways your customer service could be more inclusive and welcoming to all. 2. Share new terminology with your team for common vocabulary everyone is expected to use. 3. Ask your colleagues about their perceptions regarding your department's openness to diversity and inclusion; take their feedback and set goals for yourself and your team.

November	Positional power and unconscious bias: • Watch and discuss two videos, "Capuchin Monkeys" and "I Am Not Black; You Are Not White." • Jigsaw groups on the article, "Challenging Schema and Paradigms." • Pair-share about a time when you were in a position of power and a time when you were not, and what the impacts were on your work. • Conduct group activity on acknowledging White privilege and breaking down barriers for others.	1. Document an experience you have or witness within the next month that illustrates power dynamics or unconscious bias and how you addressed it. 2. Post a personal message on your department's website that shares your commitment to inclusivity and cultural competencies. 3. Begin to develop a list of resources that can be used with principals and teachers. 4. Read chapters 1–3 of *White Fragility* by Robin DiAngelo (2018) prior to the next session.
December	Culturally sensitive approaches to problem solving: • Watch video, "Stuck on an Elevator." • Individually respond to Circumstances, Climate, Context chart and do whip around with the whole group to share thoughts. • Conduct paired group tuning protocol on a problem of practice. • Identify and prioritize inclusive practices for the entire school or district to engage in.	1. Discuss results from the Circumstances, Climate, Context activity with your staff. 2. Teach staff how to use the tuning protocol to solve department problems. 3. Send out anonymous poll to collect feedback on how your leadership has changed or evolved over the past five months.
January	Celebrating our progress: • Have a mid-year self-reflection on new leadership competencies and growth. • Come to consensus on key training focus areas for February through June. • Create strategic planning timeline and benchmarks for execution of cultural competency work in the district next year.	

Figure 8.2: Sample district leadership professional development and action steps.

Reinforcement of learning, expansion of knowledge, and practice of job-embedded skills, rather, are the keys to making the new learning "stick." That is why stage 9, implement the initiative, is not the time to let up focus on the new initiative, but to continue to teach, train, tutor, and trust the rest of the process to secure the new initiative's success.

STAGE 8 ACTION PLAN: CHECKLIST AND REPRODUCIBLES

The following checklist and reproducibles help you apply what you learned in this chapter and move forward to the next stage of the initiative implementation process.

- ☐ Map out your long-term plan for cohesive, differentiated, and ongoing professional development in the first six months to year of implementation (see figure 8.2, page 122).

- ☐ Plan for your initiative's professional development experiences using the "Professional Development Design Worksheet" reproducible.

- ☐ Use the "Agenda-Planning Form" reproducible (page 128) to ensure the three Rs (rigor, relevance, and relationships) are well-balanced and attended to, as demonstrated in figure 8.1 (page 120).

Professional Development Design Worksheet

Directions: This worksheet is intended to ensure a well-rounded educational experience for your teachers and staff. Complete each prompt with your team for planning your professional development.

Prompts for Key Features of Design: Team Response

Content Focused
1. Content or concepts to deliver:
 	
2. The learning objectives are:
 	
3. The majority of participants are likely to:
   a. Be familiar with the topic or content
   b. Be somewhat knowledgeable
   c. Not have any experience with it
4. On a scale of 1–5, the concepts are easy (1) or difficult (5) to grasp: 1 2 3 4 5

Active Learning 1. We will actively engage participants at a minimum of every fifteen to twenty minutes by: 2. The three different interactive methods we will use to involve the audience in higher-level learning activities are: 3. The formative assessments we will use to check for understanding are:

Prompts for Key Features of Design: Team Response

Job-Embedded Collaboration

1. We will connect the participants' learning in the session to their daily work by:

2. What participants learn in the session will be reinforced on the job in the following ways:

3. We will ensure that participants will have opportunities to collaborate in between trainings by:

Models

We will employ the following demonstrations, case studies, or scenarios to illustrate key learning objectives.

1. Our exemplars have been screened in the following ways to ensure that they are free from bias, stereotypes, and discrimination of students, families, or employee groups:

2. We will invite participants to connect their own real-life work situations with the demonstrated models by:

Coaching and Support

1. We will provide instructional coaches or other expert support:
    a. Prior to the professional development session
    b. During the professional development session
    c. After the professional development session

2. Our coaches and experts will be available to help participants by:

3. Technical support will be provided by the _____ departments in the following ways:

Feedback and Reflection

1. At the beginning of the session, we will ask participants to share with us:

2. At a mid-point in the session, we will ask for feedback on:

3. After the session, we will use the following tool to reflect on strengths and weaknesses and plan next steps:

Sustained Duration

1. This professional development is most appropriately delivered:
    a. In a single session for a heterogeneous audience
    b. In several sessions for a heterogeneous audience
    c. In a single session differentiated by skill/knowledge/specialized groups
    d. In several sessions differentiated by skill/knowledge/specialized groups
    e. Other:

2. How long will it generally take for most participants to gain mastery over the subject or content?

3. We will revisit and reinforce the content throughout the school year through these means:

Agenda-Planning Form

Directions: List the topic of the agenda item in the left-hand column. In the process column, write the method or methods you would like to use to deliver the information for each item and how they connect with one or more of the three Rs. When completing the time column, remember to keep most activities under twenty minutes to maintain focus and attention span throughout.

Agenda Item	Process (Relevance, Rigor, Relationships)	Time

CHAPTER 9

Stage 9: Implement the Initiative

Congratulations! The new initiative has now marched through all the preliminary stages to ready it for full implementation. All along, you have been refining the project and making adjustments in response to feedback and data collected. By the time the initiative gets to stage 9, it should be widely known and anticipated throughout the school or district. The people involved in executing it will have been adequately trained and informed; those who aren't directly impacted will also have an awareness of its place in the fabric of the district.

That said, in some ways, the implementation stage can reflect the pilot phase in stage 4, but on a much grander scale. Although many of the kinks have been worked out, new users will experience some of the same growing pains as the first-wave users who participated in the pilot. The professional development provided will bolster everyone's capabilities, but the real apprenticeship takes place in the work environment. Educators, support staff, administrators, and students will often learn side by side through the early weeks and months of the implementation.

You can lower anxiety and fear of the unknown by emphasizing that baby steps are all that's expected at first. Soliciting, listening to, and responding immediately to feedback are crucial actions. At the first signs of discontent, frustration, or criticism, you must get at the source of these responses. Do participants require more training? Do they require additional materials or resources? Expert guidance? Communication tools? Time? You might need to slow down implementation needs, or you might need to deploy a particular type of support to the school sites. Diagnosing the problems accurately is essential.

An initiative that has had the appropriate runway to deployment should have responses to any foreseeable issues at the ready. Time is of the essence. Any perception that leadership is not able to immediately provide support, or that the district office doesn't know what it's doing, bitters the initiative faster than anything. If such toxicity spreads, it's that much harder to get everything back on track. People will generally allow a grace period when trying something new, but if repeated difficulties occur without sufficient resolutions, then the implementation could face abandonment. Even if you can't resolve problems right away, overtly communicating that you're working it out can ease tensions immensely.

This chapter illustrates how the previous eight stages have created the conditions for a confident launch and also what to do when the conditions aren't so ideal. This is the pivotal stage in the process in which all the groundwork lays a solid foundation for a permanent shift in process, practice, or policy for the present and the future.

ASSESSMENT AND ACCOUNTABILITY

As an achievement measurement, the National Implementation Research Network (n.d.), purports that:

> When 50% of the staff are using the innovation fully and effectively, it is legitimate to anticipate robust recipient outcomes. At this point, there is no doubt that the innovation is in place and is being used as intended across a site. Full Implementation creates the opportunity to see if the innovations/practices/systems are producing the anticipated outcomes. During this stage, it is appropriate to analyze the results from the selected or created assessments for individual outcomes coupled with implementation fidelity checks. Based on the results of this evaluation process, action plans are created or updated (e.g., reporting to stakeholders, celebrations, re-examination of drivers). Sustainability requires tenacity.

The goal, of course, should be higher than 50 percent of the intended employees that agree to and embrace the new initiative in order to ensure equity for all students, no matter to which teacher or school they are assigned.

According to Lyon (2017):

> Implementation is a lengthy and iterative process that involves planning, service integration, post-training support, evaluation, and collaborative problem solving. Sustaining buy-in across multiple levels of school leadership and stakeholders can produce the long term dedication that is needed to successfully implement innovative practice for student mental health. (p. 8)

Depending on the district's culture and history, however, an administrator may or may not be able to dictate usage. In actuality, there will be an implementation continuum that ranges from passive or active resistance on one end to fully committed to the innovation on the other extreme. You may determine this range through self-assessments, data collection on usage, or observations of the implementation in action. The "Self-Assessment and Rating Scale Continuum" reproducible (page 140) can help the team determine the level of staff investment in the initiative at the school or district level any given point in time.

CASE STUDY

Wellness Centers

In response to community needs, an urban district decides to establish wellness centers at its high schools. Overall student attendance had been flagging recently; those who are coming to school seem to be spending a lot of time out of class in the counseling, nurse's, and principal's offices. When surveyed, students report extremely high stress levels, along with anxiety and depression. There are also indications of poor nutrition and sleep habits. Teachers observe that students are falling asleep in class and eating junk food for breakfast. Parents also claim that their children's behaviors at home seem to be escalating, especially with dependency on video games. It is clear to everyone that the students need help.

Educators are keenly aware that education exceeds the academics, and that they are responsible for supporting students in their social-emotional growth and coping skills as well.

The leadership team researches similar districts that have successfully installed wellness centers in the area. From the variety of models, members decide to include the following services in their district: individual and group counseling, nutrition and health education, cognitive behavioral support, peer relationship skills, grief and loss management, addiction treatment, and parent-child communications. They notice that creating a warm and welcoming environment which appeals to teenagers is also a key component to exemplary programs. They map out a plan, location, and design to pilot one wellness center at their continuation high school.

After several months, the team analyzes its data related to student attendance, attentiveness in class, parent focus group feedback, and number of drop-ins at the center. The results are astounding. Improved behaviors are evident in all areas of physical, social, and emotional health. While at first students were skeptical of the center, within a matter of weeks the number of visits increased exponentially and, at a certain point, they outgrew their original space and had to expand to an adjoining room. In addition to addressing students' varying concerns, an unexpected yet welcomed bonus from the program is growth in trusting adolescent-adult relationships at the school overall.

At the end of the pilot period, the staff showcase their center by holding an open house for the rest of the district community to attend. Duly impressed, the community wholeheartedly backs expanding the initiative to the rest of the high schools. After following the next stages in the protocol, wellness centers are implemented at the beginning of the next school year at all designated sites. The district leadership team make frequent stops at each center to observe how things are going and problem solve any issues.

Based on data collected from the observational tool illustrated in figure 9.1, the team finds that additional professional development is needed for the staff, who primarily have been doing academic counseling with students up to this point. The counselors and teachers desire more training on emotional and mental health support strategies and receive release days to work with an external expert to gain those skills.

And as other gaps are noted, such as the designated space becoming quickly outgrown once word of mouth spreads about the center and students increase their visitations by over 40 percent, leaders responded in kind.

Although designed as an observation tool for the wellness center scenario, figure 9.1 is also included in a reproducible format at the end of this chapter (page 141), so you can gather relevant information for your own purposes.

Location: Wellness Center at Western High School
Observers: Student Health Coordinator and Director of Student Services
Date and Time: April 15 @12:35 p.m.
Purpose of Visit: Observation of Drop-in Wellness Center

Observation Criteria	Disagree	Neutral	Agree	Not Observed
The facility is adequate for the number of students and activities offered.	X			
The center is well-organized, clean, and inviting.			X	
The center offers appropriate and engaging resources ready for student use.			X	
The center is designed with student-friendly décor and comfortable furniture.		X		
Procedures, norms, and expectations are clearly displayed in the room.		X		
Staff show genuine interest in students' well-being and social-emotional growth.			X	
Staff utilizes positive reinforcement to encourage appropriate behavior.				X
Students interact supportively with one another in the space.			X	
Sign-in sheets for visits maintain confidentiality of students.	X			
Information is openly displayed for helplines, hotlines, or other outside wellness resources.		X		

Identified needs	How we propose to meet needs
Professional development and training	Hire outside expert to deliver workshops on social-emotional counseling.
Facility upgrade and space redesign	Contact maintenance and operations department to discuss expansion of space options.
Student safety and confidentialit	Create an area for students to sign in more confidentially via a computer kiosk instead of a clipboard.
Awareness campaign	Continue to promote awareness of the wellness center by using anonymous student testimonials.

Figure 9.1: Wellness center observation tool.

THREE SCENARIOS OF BEST-LAID PLANS

Not all implementations have the luxury of proceeding through all ten stages in the process. More often than not, when leaders change districts or promote from one job title to another, they receive an inheritance. There are decision makers who came before us, just as after we exit our positions, others will be the beneficiaries or debtors of our own choices. There is rarely a clean slate. The following three scenarios illustrate this point, and all require intervention for improvement. The circumstances call for a keen analysis of the current reality and a way to forge ahead.

SCENARIO 1: THE CHALLENGE AND INTERVENTION

A new assistant superintendent learns on day one of the job that the transition to standards-based report cards has lacked proper professional development and communication to teachers and parents. The learning objectives on the report cards themselves are problematic, and there is much dispute about the number-based rating scales. Teachers are supposed to use these report cards in a matter of months. Knowing there is a brewing controversy, how does the assistant superintendent proceed?

This district charges the new assistant superintendent with executing an initiative she didn't author, nor feels is ready for prime time. The warning signs for disaster are all there. She must figure out how to navigate the tricky territory of honoring those who have invested years in the development of this initiative and are ready to go full steam ahead and those who seem completely blindsided by the initiative.

First, she solicits the help of the teachers' association president to send out a survey and identify the main pain points. Then she holds three open forums for teachers around the district to make sure she truly understands their concerns. After reviewing the data from the survey and listening tour, the new assistant superintendent's instructional services team makes the call: six of the eighteen schools that are ready to implement the report card right away will do so as a pilot that fall and spring.

Simultaneously, she assembles a report card team with parents, students, teachers, and administrators to evaluate and come to a consensus on which criteria to include. She will plan professional development along with frequent communications to prepare everyone for a full-scale launch the following school year.

SCENARIO 2: THE CHALLENGE AND INTERVENTION

A new principal starts in November at an alternative secondary school where the former principal has been demoted to a teaching position . . . at the same site. The accreditation commission has given the school one year to improve in several key areas or risk losing its status as an acceptable pathway to higher education. The staff is used to delivering packet work with very little direct instruction. How does the principal modify the preexisting culture and raise the bar for student learning to meet the requirements?

The principal in this unenviable position, who ascends his former superior and needs several quick wins to avoid school disaccreditation, must tread lightly while also asserting a critical call for action with his staff. With little time to build the relationships that would normally precede such monumental change, he reserves a full-day retreat with his staff to do some team building, affirm their history and background, and validate and appreciate them for serving the most disadvantaged students in the district.

Instead of hitting the accreditation team's many critiques of the school head on, he asks the staff how they desire to improve their systems and practices. During the self-reflection process, they report that they want some adaptations in their curriculum offerings and recognize that their students need to be more actively involved. Seeing some overlap, the new principal helps them connect their own hopes for the school with the committee's recommendations.

He proclaims, "They can either do this *to* us, or we can tell them what *we're* going to do instead." By transferring the agency to his staff, they work together to begin co-creating solutions to make their work more fulfilling as well as satisfy the accreditation team—not to mention, improve students' lives even more. They put together an action plan that all of them can get behind and submit it to the commission for approval.

SCENARIO 3: THE CHALLENGE AND INTERVENTION

A district hires a new director of special education after the former beloved director of ten years decides to retire. The reason he was so beloved? The six program specialists under him were calling all the shots, some of which have contributed to an almost $35 million budget deficit in the district. The superintendent tasks the new director with pulling in the reins and reducing costs by 20 percent within the fiscal year and another 20 percent the following year. This means evaluating resource allocations, staffing, and services to families. How does the new director do so in a way that maintains morale while substantially challenging past practice?

The new special education director wants to do right by the students as well as restore a balanced budget. She must seriously question the practices that got the department into such a deficit in the first place. Her staff is incredibly sensitive to the perception that they are not managing district resources well and get extremely defensive when the superintendent explains that they must remain cost neutral and will not receive additional funding for staffing until they redesign their programs for efficiency and effectiveness. Not only does the director have to buffer the feelings of her staff but also earn the trust of her superintendent.

Digging deeper into the data, she discovers that the business department, human resources, and instructional services are all using different systems to account for expenditures, and the numbers vary widely. There are huge discrepancies between the staffing allocations and how many open job positions exist. The human resources database shows several closed positions toward which business services is still allocating funding in the budget. Furthermore, the director realizes that her own special education staff have been hiring instructional aides without anyone's knowledge. She confides this information to the superintendent, who takes charge from there, recognizing that the problem is far bigger than one department. The superintendent meets with senior management and has the assistant superintendents over each division create checks and balances that will clean up past practices and establish new protocols going forward.

HOW TO MOVE FORWARD

None of these situations is easy or clear-cut; truly, there are no right or wrong answers. But there are pros and cons to any approach. Those initiatives we inherit are a bit of a different animal than those we develop from scratch. Damage control is sometimes the operating system needed when stepping into an initiative already underway. When crafting one's own initiative, however, you can avoid many pitfalls by following the series of preplanned stages outlined in this book.

Another relevant example is the sudden conversion to full distance education classes in reaction to the COVID-19 pandemic in 2020. The stages leading up to implementation were vastly abbreviated, and districts could not invest much time, if any, on the planning, piloting, and data analysis portions of the process. Without the benefits of those early steps, schools found themselves in the position of having to make major shifts in instruction regardless of readiness.

If a school or district must skip the first seven stages due to uncontrollable circumstances, or when a leader inherits a poorly executed initiative that's already been left foundering in the field, it must place heavy and pronounced focus on the professional development, implementation, and ongoing support stages. If there is even a little bit of time to plan ahead, the school or district must make every effort to create accessible, meaningful, and differentiated training offerings. It's well worth using all resources available to entice people to participate to get up to speed, including additional pay or other types of incentives.

When schools across the world shut down in the spring of 2020, many educators had less than a week's notice to shift instructional modes from the classroom to distance or hybrid learning settings. According to an interactive map from Our World in Data (https://bit.ly/2UeItKv), by May 2020 only two nations on the globe (Belarus and Tajikistan) had zero restrictions on schooling. The rest of the countries had either recommended or required closures.

At the time, many educators thought it would be a two-week quarantine window, and then all would return to normal. As the pandemic unfolded, two weeks became a month, which then became an unspecified return as they drifted into summer. Soon it became obvious that K–12 education would be going through a fast-forwarded evolution like never before. While pockets of schools and districts were fully prepared to go online, most were far from it. They were all simultaneously thrust into the implementation stage of virtual instruction, ready or not.

When facing a novel situation such as this, you can condense the first six stages of the new initiative process into two phases. The first phase is gathering together a think tank of district leaders, employee group representatives, teachers, counselors, parents, students, board members, and support staff who all bring unique perspectives to the flash brainstorming session. In the meeting, the team identifies the multiple factors affecting families, students, and employees. You might also develop some solutions within the conversation, but you will work out specific details in phase two.

You then charge the larger body representing each stakeholder group with creating a plan to execute its particular assignments. Each think tank representative becomes a team leader and develops strategies and approaches to meet each challenge head on. Figure 9.2 demonstrates how phase two will commence.

Think Tank Representative	Challenge	Assignment
Student Body President	Students may be feeling anxious or depressed about missing many important events like prom and graduation. Students will no longer have in-person connections with adults or peers. Students need a social-emotional support system while sheltering in place.	Hold virtual meeting with all schools' student leadership teams to discuss student needs. Report back to district counselors and student support services on key concerns. Develop online resources for students to access remotely (counseling, crisis lines, contact info for staff). Come up with alternatives to traditional events for social outlets.
Education Foundation President	Students from low socioeconomic households may not have devices or internet access. The achievement and equity gap will increase in this environment if we don't find ways to reach out to needy students.	Put together a campaign for technology donations or fundraising to buy Chromebooks for all students who qualify for free and reduced-price meals. Work with other community organizations to collect food, clothing, and other goods for families in need.
Assistant Superintendent of Human Resources	Teachers haven't been expected to deliver instruction other than in a traditional classroom until now; they will need training. We will need to collaborate with each of the employee unions to outline new duties.	Work with the assistant superintendent of instruction to develop guidelines for e-learning. Reach out to union leadership to create memoranda of understanding (MOUs) that reflect new work environments and expectations.
Food Nutrition Services Manager	Even though schools are closed, we still need to find ways to feed students who qualify for free and reduced-price meals. Since we're already operating at a deficit, we should see if there is funding available for support.	Identify three centralized locations in the city where students can pick up breakfast and lunch. Apply for state and federal meals grants to fund efforts. Communicate with local volunteers to help coordinate meal pick up and drop off.

Figure 9.2: Stakeholder representative assignments.   continued ▶

Think Tank Representative	Challenge	Assignment
Director of Instructional Technology	Ensure that all students have computers and internet access. Students need to know how to get online and participate in classwork and virtual activities. We will need to find out if students are still going to be participating in standardized assessments.	Inventory devices across sites and deploy computers and hotspots to students who need them. Work with local internet and cable companies for discounted rates for families and homes. Work with the curriculum department to develop instructions and tutorials for students using online platforms.
Board Member	Closing schools will affect other city services, like the library, recreation, and police, so coordinating with them is important. We will need to make sure we don't lose daily attendance funding or other resources from the state if our students can't return to school.	The board of trustees will reach out to the city council and mayor to find out what work could be shared. Board members will also send letters and lobby to local and state politicians to make sure we aren't penalized financially for lack of student attendance this spring.

In extreme cases like a pandemic, the whole education institution is forced to deviate from current operating procedures and refocus all efforts on the urgency of the situation. Rocketing directly into the implementation stage just means that you will spend more time simultaneously covering the bases of earlier steps: communicating, engaging, experiencing trial and error, collecting data, interpreting results, and teaching and reteaching staff. It's trickier but unavoidable. The implementation will include securing the basic resources, initiating people to the so-called new normal, and doing the best we can today, and then better tomorrow, until we are fully acclimated.

CONCLUSION

Implementation itself is a complex stage, even when not in crisis mode. When a new initiative makes it to this step, the intention is that it makes a positive impact on student learning, has lasting power, and indelibly changes the school or district for the greater good. After a while, it becomes such a part of the school or district's identity that people can't remember when it didn't exist. There is satisfaction in that, but also a looming danger if ongoing support is not provided and those new to the institution don't understand the *why* behind it. The final stage in the initiative implementation process addresses the imperative obligation and commitment to keeping the initiative alive and well, even after it isn't new anymore.

STAGE 9 ACTION PLAN: CHECKLIST AND REPRODUCIBLES

The following checklist and reproducibles help you apply what you learned in this chapter and move forward to the next stage of the initiative implementation process.

- ☐ Complete and apply the "Self-Assessment and Rating Scale Continuum" reproducible (page 140) to the initiative during the early part of stage 9.

- ☐ When conducting observations of the implementation in action, adapt the "Implementation Observation Tool" reproducible (page 141) to fit your particular circumstances.

- ☐ Use the "Stakeholder Representative Assignments" reproducible (page 142) for identifying and assigning appropriate roles and outreach mechanisms. See figure 9.2 (page 137) for an example.

Self-Assessment and Rating Scale Continuum

Directions: A quick questionnaire to gather input from those implementing the initiative can create a snapshot of how the process is going by using a simple five-question rating scale with sentence frames. After collecting a statistically significant sample size, the team leader can then apply the individual responses to the continuum and see how the curve plays out through the school or district.

On a scale from 1–10 (low to high), indicate your level of agreement with each of the following statements on the product, practice, or process your district recently adopted.	
I use this product, practice, or process on a (regular, daily, or weekly) basis.	1 2 3 4 5 6 7 8 9 10
I understand the benefits of this product, practice, or process on (student learning, employee productivity, or family well-being).	1 2 3 4 5 6 7 8 9 10
I know why the district adopted this product, practice, or process and see how it is improving the (learning or work environment).	1 2 3 4 5 6 7 8 9 10
I believe that this product, practice, or process supports us in achieving our school or district's (mission, vision, or goals).	1 2 3 4 5 6 7 8 9 10
I could not do my job as effectively without this product, practice, or process.	1 2 3 4 5 6 7 8 9 10
Total:	__ /50 points

10 percent	30 percent	50 percent	70 percent	90 percent
Noncompliance	Duty	Acceptance	Commitment	Fidelity
(0–14 points)	(15–24 points)	(25–34 points)	(35–44 points)	(45–50 points)

Implementation Observation Tool

Directions: Create observation criteria that pertain to your implementation in the first column. When conducting the walkthrough, have observers write down their assessment as to what degree the criteria are being met. In the bottom section, identify supports and action steps that will address identified needs.

Location:
Observer:
Date and Time:
Purpose of Visit:

Observation Criteria	Disagree	Neutral	Agree	Not Observed
Engagement or participation:				
Relationships:				
Techniques or strategies:				
Organization and structures:				
Objectives and goals:				
Consistency of practices:				
General feedback:				

Identified needs:	How we propose to meet needs:
Professional development and training:	
Facilities:	
Student support:	
Staff support:	
Materials, technology, and resources:	
Awareness and communications:	
Other:	

Leading the Launch © 2022 Solution Tree Press • SolutionTree.com
Visit **go.SolutionTree.com/leadership** to download this page.

Stakeholder Representative Assignments

Directions: Select a representative from each part of the district community who agrees to interface with a larger group of constituents they serve or are connected with. At a minimum, parents, students, teachers, and support staff should all have a place at the table. Depending on the nature or extent of the crisis, the leadership team leader may also want to include others such as emergency personnel, social services, or community organization leaders. Use the prompts in the first row to help think-tank members develop their responses, approaches, and strategies.

Think Tank Representative	Challenge	Assignment
Name: Title: Organization: Position: Contact information:	From my perspective . . . An obstacle we might need to address is . . . I think we need to better understand . . . Maybe we should consider . . .	I will . . . I know . . . I am connected to . . . I have resources for . . . I can commit to . . .

CHAPTER 10

Stage 10: Provide Ongoing Support

Don't stop short! The leadership team remains responsible for keeping a clear focus on the program, project, or service they've worked so hard to implement. It can be tempting for a school or district to move on to the next new initiative and let enthusiasm wane for existing ones. Just because it's now become a standard operating procedure in the district does not mean that the leadership team can stop nurturing it. The team should preschedule benchmarks, briefings, and evaluation tools to monitor progress and exhibit commitment to the sanctioned course of action. This chapter also focuses on setting up checks and balances to sustain implementation, recognizing when interventions or extensions are needed, and how to weed out practices that are no longer productive. Kathleen Ryan Jackson, Dean Fixsen, and Caryn Ward published a 2018 study on school turnaround efforts and found the following compelling evidence:

> With the support of skilled teams who focus on implementation, districts can expect 80% successful use of effective practices in about 3 years (Chamberlain, Brown, & Saldana, 2011; Fixsen et al., 2001); without the support of skilled teams who focus on implementation, districts might achieve 14% successful use of effective practices after 17 years. (Balas & Boren, 2000; Green, 2008)

Jackson and colleagues (2018) also sought to demonstrate how effective practices (*what* needs to be used and done), effective implementation (*how* systemwide supports are developed and used), and supportive contexts (*where* hospitable environments are nurtured) can result in improved "educationally significant outcomes" (p. 6). This holistic approach underscores the notion that implementation is a process, not a single event. Going into autopilot is not an option. The initiative still needs hands-on guidance and cultivation to flourish.

A CULTURE OF CONTINUED GROWTH

The principle element to ongoing support of any initiative once it's firmly established is to cultivate the culture, environment, and space for continued growth by establishing and communicating what's loose and what's tight about the implementation (DuFour, 2016). As alluded to in earlier chapters, culture trumps all. In other words, you can set whatever course you want for your business or school, but it's the people (their beliefs and behaviors) that ultimately determine what happens. Therefore, keep a keen eye on how the culture is accepting, integrating, or rejecting parts of the implementation. Strategies must include noting the habits people develop and exercise, how they respond to hardships, as well as that indecipherable quality of a particular environment.

The primary way to contend with culture is to have a steady hand in shaping it through the following approaches.

1. Continue to offer professional development, work out problems, elevate practices, communicate with stakeholders, and celebrate successes with the existing staff.

2. Onboard new employees to the systems in place, properly train them, pair them with mentors, and conduct frequent observations and check-ins.

Veteran and novice colleagues may have differing yet overlapping aspirations. Their skill sets, understanding of the implementation, and longevity may vary, but their desire to be successful, positively impact student learning, and contribute to the community are shared. You can honor their unique circumstances by differentiating support and acknowledging that not everyone is starting from the same place.

Those already working in the district when the implementation originated still need attention as they improve their skills and knowledge. By adopting a mentality that everyone in the district is a lifelong learner and providing choices for how to deepen their know-how, staff will feel both respected and galvanized. Depending on the complexity of the endeavor, encourage practitioners to strive for professional growth and expertise, even after they have mastered basic techniques or concepts. Refresher courses and advanced workshops where people earn credit or additional responsibilities may prompt staff to elevate their work.

Those who've recently joined the district won't automatically realize that the initiative has not been there all along. Make sure not to leave new hires without a coherent understanding of how the district functions and neglect to state outright its underpinning values. As mentioned previously, clarity precedes competence, and it's your job to articulate expectations in the onboarding design. Therefore, orienting new employees to the priorities of the school or district is critical.

New staff members need relevant background information, understanding of the mission and vision, and training on how to execute their duties related to the key programs. You can coordinate this through explicit instruction and frequent opportunities to learn on the job. Mentorship, coaching, and making expert help available reinforces a strong foundation as well. By pairing colleagues together, educators can apply new practices side by side and support each other in attaining proficiencies to carry out the implementation as designed.

Formal professional development is just one component of continued support. Frequent communications about the evolution of the implementation and how it is improving the performance of the district helps to keep it on the radar as well. Leadership can craft the narrative of the implementation through newsletter articles, social media blurbs, videos of it in action, website highlights, and testimonials. Improved student results or other data that tell a compelling story also sustains the efforts. It's important as well to be transparent about any alterations or adjustments made due to possible obstacles encountered throughout.

It's important to view initiative implementation as a living, breathing organism that changes when the conditions call for it. Continually managing expectations and responding to the environmental state of affairs will help sustain the initiative for the long term.

This hearkens back to DuFour's (2016) work on loose and tight culture for PLCs. He states, "Think of *tight* as synonymous with *nondiscretionary*. Think of *loose* as the equivalent of *empowered to make decisions*" (p. 33). There may be an ebb and flow of what's loose as long as everyone is clear on what's tight and operates within those boundaries.

CASE STUDY

Professional Learning Communities

A mid-sized suburban school district is in the process of implementing the PLC process. While student achievement in the district has been outstanding thus far, the superintendent takes the stance that there is always room to grow, especially as teachers are still working on integrating state standards and instructional materials in their classrooms. Leadership set up the scaffolding for two years prior to this initiative by introducing weekly collaboration time in the schedule, sending many staff to PLC conferences, and developing a training-of-trainers model, in which teachers were trained offsite and returned to their campuses to train others. Ultimately, staff agreed to make a laser-like commitment to ensure that every student in every classroom would experience meaningful learning through relevant opportunities and thoughtful discussions.

The PLC process recognizes that the key to improved learning for students is continuous job-embedded learning for educators (DuFour et al., 2016). The district committed to providing professional development, time, and resources, as well as collecting feedback to guide its course over the next several years. The superintendent clearly communicated that becoming a districtwide PLC does not happen overnight. It takes a lot of planning and cannot happen without ongoing support for all involved in the process. Furthermore, PLCs are not a program to be adopted, but a *way of being* to be developed through authentic collaborative work.

Although this communication from the top trickled down to everyone in the district, it was vague enough that the leadership team soon started hearing ripples of discontent at different school sites. The teachers' union president shared with the assistant superintendent of instruction that certain principals were rigidly applying the criteria outlined in their collectively bargained memorandum of understanding (MOU) to teams at their sites, while others were being more flexible.

Tapping relative research on schools that have successfully implemented the PLC process, they learned the importance of communicating clearly to staff at every level. As Jackson and colleagues (2018) note, it's necessary for implementation teams to:

> Establish communication loops to ensure they are communicating relevant information to one another as needed (daily, weekly, monthly) from practice-level staff to implementation teams to executive leadership. In this way, impediments and gaps in support at the classroom and school level can be "lifted up" to those who can solve these bigger problems that stand in the way of turnaround for all schools in the state. These practice-policy communication loops (Fixsen et al., 2013; Sterman, 2006; Svensson, Tomson, & Rindzeviciute, 2017) are the basis for changing current policies, procedures, funding strategies, structures, roles, and functions to more precisely and purposefully focus on improving student outcomes and closing achievement gaps. (p. 31)

The teachers' union president and the assistant superintendent of instruction decide to collaborate on a joint memo to send out to all employees sharing adjustments they will make. The purpose of the letter, shown in figure 10.1, is to acknowledge the problems being experienced as well as how they would cooperate in solving them.

FROM: Superintendent and Teachers' Association President

RE: Professional Learning Communities Update

Dear Colleagues:

Over the past two years, the educators' association and district management have embarked together on recognizing and valuing the time spent working with colleagues. Last year, it was in the form of collaboration, which was pretty open-ended. This year, it has been to establish the PLC process in our district, which encompasses focusing on what students need to know, whether they have learned it, and what interventions and enrichments need to be in place to support student learning.

In a district of this size, this has been a tall order. We acknowledge that after laying the groundwork last year, this first full year of implementation has seen both successes and growing pains that we need to address. We all agree that student learning is our top priority and focus, and we've all witnessed that early efforts have begun to yield positive impacts in the classroom, increased collegiality and collaboration, and professional growth for the entire district.

The words we wrote in our first joint memo together last spring remain true. Rest assured, this is not one of those educational "flavors of the month" we've all likely experienced. The district is fully committed to sustaining the PLC process for the long term. Also rest assured that this will not be a one-size-fits-all model. While the elements, themes, and topics will be guided by the instructional services department, we encourage each school site to fashion its own PLC, reflective of the unique natures of our schools.

Simply put, the district will provide the *what*, which is a clear focus on the four critical questions of a PLC, and guidance on collaboration processes. You may see this in the negotiated memorandum of understanding (MOU) with our teachers' association. Educators, however, will provide the *how*, including instructional strategies they choose, assessments they develop, and topics they discuss to move student learning forward.

Senior management and the educators' association leadership have been meeting regularly since July to ensure that we follow the intent of the MOU, educators feel supported in this work, and the long-term plans for building PLCs at the school sites remains a positive experience. In addition, we have met with focus groups, heard from site reps at the rep council, listened to concerns brought through site liaison committees, and reviewed the recent PLC survey.

Life does not always fall in line with the good intentions set forth; therefore, the instructional services team will be adjusting the implementation approach in response to feedback from educators. The two key topics that we clearly need to address include the following.

1. The amount of paperwork and products generated by and expected from collaborative teams
2. Scheduling, frequency, and logistics of team meetings

Instructional services leadership in conjunction with site principals are addressing the first item immediately. Instructional services and site administrators will be looking at what's expected and calibrating to make sure that the paperwork and products are meaningful, manageable, and reasonable across all schools. We all agree that the most important work product and purpose of establishing PLCs is improved student learning.

We will address the second topic will via the union-district bargaining process in early spring. The educators' association will survey members in December about future collaborative time for the bargaining unit. We will use survey information, plus anecdotal feedback at site visits, the rep council, and communication to leadership to prioritize interests at the bargaining table.

Figure 10.1: Districtwide joint memo on PLCs.

continued ▶

> We believe we can best achieve all of us working together for the common good for all students through the PLC process. The district remains committed to providing high-quality training, support, and flexibility to get us through the bumpy patches these first few years until the PLC process becomes a natural part of how we operate. We are here to listen, either directly or through site reps, adjust as needed, and help implement the current PLC MOU in the best way possible.
>
> Thank you for your authentic input, and we will continue to travel this road together and be united in our shared goals.

The assistant superintendent follows up by holding a principals' meeting to calibrate how site administrators are interpreting the MOU as well as their grasp of the spirit of the implementation. They come up with a list of activities that teams could engage in that would help roll out the operation more consistently across all of the schools.

She then shares the list with the union president, who tweaks some of the language to improve understanding. Finally, the assistant superintendent emails the list to instructional staff so everyone will be in better alignment and have clarity about the tight and loose parameters.

This scenario illustrates the type of work that takes place in stage 10. It's about educating the people involved in the implementation, making sure they are equipped with the tools and knowledge necessary to carry it out, and addressing the gaps that need filling when they inevitably occur.

ASSISTANCE AND SUPPORT

Ongoing assistance should not just be offered to staff, but also to students, parents, or others affected by the operation. Identify what they will need to be successful participating in the program, service, or project. Consider material accommodations, especially if the initiative requires special technologies or tools that families don't always have access to. Use similar approaches for onboarding staff with other users, including frequent communications, tutorials, informational meetings, and guidance. Differentiate these approaches according to the audience to increase accessibility and familiarity with the implementation in appropriate ways. Depending on who is impacted the most, tailor your methods with more or less information and instruction.

Keep the big picture and the smaller details in mind simultaneously by developing a steering guide to provide a health check on the initiative through benchmarks at selected intervals. The term *steering* is deliberate to emphasize two actions: (1) drive strategic direction and (2) supervise the overall implementation. Later, you can use the "Steering Guide for Monitoring Progress" reproducible (page 153) as an open-ended planning chart to monitor progress throughout the term of the implementation.

This final stage concludes the new initiative implementation process. Continual care and feeding will help cement the district's investment and endure the test of time. The implementation has now settled into the bedrock and become a significant part of how work is conducted in the school or district. Not all initiatives are meant to last forever, however, so evaluating your initiative's effectiveness throughout is an important part of what follows. The last thing you want is for a program to become stale and ineffective but remain perennially due to inertia or lack of imagination. Sometimes you can revive energy into an existing system, and sometimes it deserves a proper burial. Regardless, it's the leader's role to attend to his or her initiative throughout its natural lifespan.

UNPRODUCTIVE PRACTICES

Although it's not an official part of the initiative implementation process, it's worth spending some time on how to terminate initiatives that have outlived their usefulness. The intentional practice of rebalancing the workload and number of responsibilities allows the district to focus its resources and energies in more manageable ways. Sometimes what was once deemed innovative at an earlier time is no longer cutting edge and could be replaced by a more efficient or effective system. It may be that the initiative never yielded the hoped-for results, or that it even hindered forward progress. Looking at existing endeavors with a critical eye keeps them fresh and creates the opportunity to readjust or resign the operation entirely.

The initiative prioritization rubric in figure 3.2 (page 39) lists all the major district undertakings and where they are in their implementation. Leaders should periodically consult this document with a diverse team of people who are familiar with the various projects. Much like in the original prioritizing procedure, every item is evaluated for its impact on student learning and overall good of the school or district. A rating scale to determine whether to eliminate programs, projects, and services, such as the one in the "Initiative Assessment Tool" reproducible (page 154), may assist the leadership team in objectively determining which and whether to discontinue.

Once a vestige of the past is deemed no longer productive, it's a good idea to consult with stakeholders about eliminating it. There will be those who are reluctant to see it go, simply because it's easy and comfortable, and others who are downright upset because they hold a fierce allegiance to it. Just as in stage 5, engagement is necessary to gather input from stakeholders on the potential effects of suspending the initiative. Even if the outreach doesn't change the outcome, it may provide leadership with some additional steps to take that can ease the transition. Communicating the rationale and process for sunsetting the plan and what will replace it is also key. District staff, parents and families, and students will need to know that the call to cease the initiative has been carefully and considerately made.

Some former practices will be automatically supplanted as by-products of a new initiative, while others must be addressed by themselves. Digitization long ago replaced preparing students for work on the assembly line, but there are still some industrial models hanging on in our educational system. At times, a district is forced to relinquish an outdated system simply because the product doesn't exist anymore. The textbooks are out of print; the software is no longer supported; or the supplier has gone out of business.

It may not be easy to convince staff to let go of inefficient practices, even if it's obvious that the new way will reduce redundancies and produce better outcomes. What someone already knows how to do may undercut learning a new system that would save time and energy. Another hurdle might be the perception or reality that human resources are being displaced by machines. What it currently takes three employees to do could be automated instead, but leaders often face the political and social obstacles of reducing staff.

We can also apply the three orders of barriers to change defined in the introduction to the cancellation of any antiquated method (see page 5). First-order barriers (equipment, resources, and support) may come in the form of "Don't take away my . . . I can't work without it." The ellipses might represent any current tool or method the person is using—an email service, a software program, or a brand of device. Second-order barriers (knowledge, skills, beliefs, and attitudes) exhibit themselves in the mindsets expressed about the change. For example, "I don't believe in [this shift], and in my experience [that new thing] won't work." Third-order barriers (institutional structures) can present themselves as "We don't have enough [time, money, people, or resources] to stop doing [this] or start doing [that]." Barriers to innovation are potent, and we must attend to them.

For example, many districts have increasingly shifted from manual data entry to online platforms or software. A new student information system (SIS) may include ways for parents to register their children via the internet, administrators to create master schedules, school offices to communicate with families through portals, and teachers to develop and send out report cards. Likewise, there are systems and tools for moving from paper timecards to digital ones; from hard copy newsletters sent through regular mail to web-based ones; from scheduling substitute teachers over the phone to using an online system; from filing papers in manila folders to scanning essential documents into the cloud.

There are many opportunities to shift old habits into new approaches and create more efficiency, effectiveness, and improved outcomes. The problem for the leader often becomes one of staffing. The consequence of digitizing tasks is that we now need fewer people to accomplish them. The question leaders face at this point is, which digital tools will leaders choose to utilize, and how will they balance and justify newfound efficiency with the likely reduction in staff?

Acknowledging the three orders of barriers will help unpeel the layers of opposition and give the leader insight into possible approaches. If the resistance stems from lack of materials (a first-order barrier), then it's necessary to provide the appropriate resources. If it comes from beliefs or attitudes (a second-order barrier), explaining why the change is beneficial may shed light. If it is generated from organizational structures in place (a third-order barrier), then holding a visioning session with those affected and making them part of the solution can help win people over.

Not all initiatives that face elimination should be replaced with anything at all. We must also question the policies, historical practices, traditions, and instructional activities. Public educators have long debated the worth of some of the controversial topics in the following categories.

- **Instructional:** Homework, test prep, copying down lecture notes, rote memorization, filling in worksheets, and repetition
- **Assessment:** Pop quizzes, weighted grades, zeros for not completing assignments, red ink, standardized testing, report cards, A–F grading
- **Disciplinary:** Suspensions for truancy, recess detention, dress codes or school uniforms, zero tolerance for drugs or violence, cell phone bans, Saturday school
- **Organizational:** Bell schedules, busing, hall passes, bathroom permissions, school start and end times, desks in rows
- **Traditions:** Science fairs, spelling bees, talent contests, pep rallies, assemblies, school rivalries, homecoming court
- **Stratification:** Ability grouping; academic (basic, college prep, honors) and vocational tracking; retention for failure; gifted and talented education; special education; language, racial, and social inequities; class rankings

This is not to say that any of the practices in the list are right or wrong, but that it's valuable to examine whether they are perpetuating systems that hurt more than help students. Depending on the community, some may be untouchable, but starting the conversation can plant seeds for progress beyond the status quo.

Even instructional techniques can create serious debate. For example, is it still worth teaching cursive? Does sustained silent reading result in improved comprehension? Will the five-paragraph essay enhance or stilt written expression? Should students copy definitions from the dictionary to learn new vocabulary words? And what about grammar drills, sentence diagramming, and error correction exercises?

Mathematics, social studies, and other content areas aren't immune to the debates. Do students need to memorize basic mathematics facts, dates of historical events, or the segments of the life cycle? The disputes are endless. But if we continue to adopt new programs reflecting research-based approaches without giving up the old guard, it causes dissonance for both students and teachers. That is why we need to evaluate preexisting customs and traditions as stringently as new initiatives—and retire those found wanting.

All our decisions must be motivated by the goal of meeting students' needs. Students are wired differently than those of earlier generations. Half our students were born at the same time the first iPad came out. The rest have never known a world without the internet, Google, social media, and artificial intelligence. Protecting bygone instructional models and institutional formats cannot be merely for the sake of the adults in the building. Leaders have to create the conditions in which our thinking shifts to the outcomes our future graduates' demand and desire to inherit and shape the world awaiting them.

CONCLUSION

Ongoing support will at times have a light touch and at other times a greater emphasis. Elements from some of the earlier stages, such as build stakeholder engagement, can be utilized to check in on the implementation and identify what, if any, interventions or course corrections are required. You may find that additional messaging or a refresher professional learning session should be offered to get the initiative back in gear. The distinct goal is to not let the implementation become stagnant or less effective over time. Planning and monitoring the initiative and sharing how it's maturing along the way will help the district define and share its successes.

STAGE 10 ACTION PLAN: CHECKLIST AND REPRODUCIBLES

The following checklist and reproducibles help you apply what you learned in this chapter, the last stage of the initiative implementation process.

- ☐ Use the "Steering Guide for Monitoring Progress" reproducible to flesh out the details for your short-term, mid-term, and long-term initiative implementation plans.

- ☐ Use the "Initiative Assessment Tool" reproducible (page 154) to evaluate your existing initiatives to ascertain whether they should remain in play or be eliminated in the future.

Steering Guide for Monitoring Progress

Directions: Complete the following chart to outline your short-term, mid-term, and long-term steering plans. Examples are provided in italics to illustrate sample responses in each column.

	Short-Term Steering Plan	**Mid-Term Steering Plan**	**Long-Term Steering Plan**
What?	*Costs, benefits analysis*	*Program evaluation*	*Coherence with overarching goals*
Who?	*Curriculum and instruction department*	*District office collaboration team meeting*	*Senior cabinet and board of trustees*
How?	*Document log-ons, usage, and investments to date*	*Collect and analyze formative data*	*Review longitudinal summative assessment results*
When?	*Quarterly*	*Biannually*	*Annually*

Initiative Assessment Tool

Directions: Complete this chart for each of the current initiatives in your school or district. The point values assigned to each item determine how close the program, product, or service is to meeting school or district goals.

Key Questions	Rating Scale (low to high)
1. Is the initiative still strategically aligned to current district plans?	1 2 3 4 5
2. Has the initiative made a direct and measurable impact on student learning or employee productivity?	1 2 3 4 5
3. Has the initiative helped to close achievement gaps between student groups?	1 2 3 4 5
4. Does the initiative connect to or advance other initiatives?	1 2 3 4 5
5. Does the initiative have support from key stakeholders?	1 2 3 4 5
6. Is the initiative still relevant and meaningful for 21st century learning and work environments?	1 2 3 4 5
7. Do the benefits outweigh the fiscal investment?	1 2 3 4 5
8. Are the resources required to keep it going worth the time and energy?	1 2 3 4 5
9. Is the service, project, or program required by law or moral obligation?	1 2 3 4 5
10. If we eliminated this initiative, how significant would the opposition be?	1 2 3 4 5
Scoring Guide: 10–24 points: Eliminate the initiative. 25–39 points: Conduct more outreach and re-evaluate. 40–50 points: Keep the initiative.	

EPILOGUE

Balancing Acts

The new initiative process, while outlined in ten separate stages, is meant to allow the fluidity of spending more or less time in each phase and for them to sometimes overlap. Some stages may be more critical in certain regions than others as well. School districts with highly involved parents require more time in engagement and communications. Others might need additional time in the staff training and professional development stages. There is no exact template to follow, therefore, clustering the stages into three categories may be helpful based on their purpose.

THREE CATEGORIES FOR IMPLEMENTATION

The ten stages in the initiative implementation process can be loosely grouped into three categories based on purpose, for example: (1) research and vetting, (2) prototype and pilot, and (3) approval and implementation. Although every situation is different, and the flow through these ten stages will vary from district to district, these categories can be helpful in guiding the process.

STAGES 1–3

Stages 1–3 are largely conceptual, involving research, deep conversations with colleagues, and prioritization in relation to other district initiatives. They are designed to first examine the idea from all angles and then sift through the details before resolving where, when, and if the initiative can coexist with other programs, services, and projects in the school or district. Many, if not most, fledgling initiatives will not make it past these first three stages. They are not meant to. This part of the screening process should eliminate the bad ideas, put the OK ones on hold, and send the good ones, possibly later determined to be great, to the next three stages.

STAGES 4–6

Stages 4–6 are the trial-and-error period. The prototype and pilot are developed and tested out in the field, and then data is collected and evaluated. Choosing the right location, audience, and timing is key for the pilot to yield the desired information. Sometimes a leader will select a site that seems eager, ready, and willing, but does not reflect the greater populace that might not be as open to the innovation. If only early adopters are included in the experiment, the leader may later find that their reaction is not indicative of the majority. Instead, having a mixed stakeholder group can suss out the sticking points as people of varying abilities and mindsets encounter different kinds of problems along the way. Once the leadership team leader administers multiple measures and analyzes the results, he or she will prepare the case for the decision-making body to gain access to the concluding steps in the protocol.

STAGES 7–10

Even though stage 7 is included in the final cluster with stages 8–10, it really is a standalone that establishes the make or break point for the initiative. It serves as the gatekeeper to either rejecting the new idea, sending it back to an earlier round, or allowing it to move forward for adoption. The leader needs to produce a clear and persuasive case to the team that covers all bases and sufficiently answers all questions. Any areas that show weakness will be scrutinized and dissected to shed light on potential fatal flaws in the plan. Then the consulting team comes to consensus on whether to green-light, yellow-light, or red-light the initiative. The initiatives that pass muster will be forwarded to the final three stages.

Now that the initiative has been approved, it triggers the professional development planning and delivery, the actual implementation, and ongoing support stages. It may be tempting for a leader to be hands-off after mobilizing the initiative, but it's more important than ever to cultivate its maturation. Proper training, progress monitoring, and continual induction for newcomers and refreshers for current users all contribute to infusing the initiative into the system. Support also comes through deliberate resource allocation, inclusion into local strategic plans, and frequent updates to stakeholders. Remembering to publicly celebrate outcomes and accomplishments is just as important as the behind-the-scenes work. Initiatives that aren't placed in the limelight risk fading into obscurity after time. What we do want is for it to become ingrained in the work we do, the way we are, and what we value—without it, the school or district cannot operate at the highest level.

As mentioned in earlier chapters, whether an initiative is externally imposed by conditions not under our control and timeline or introduced to the school or district voluntarily, following the process up to the implementation launch is critical. Any under-attended stages may cause unneeded difficulty and catapult the initiative back to square one. And that's the last thing a leader hopes to experience. This is not to say there are guarantees either way, but establishing a firm foundation of support will more likely bolster success.

A common axiom used in situations in which a team is developing a plan at the same time as implementing it is *building the plane as we are flying it*. This often occurs in circumstances outside of our locus of control and requires a different operating system than chosen initiatives. While not ideal, we have to be realistic and know that we cannot plan for everything in life. The 2020 COVID-19 pandemic is a perfect example of this phenomenon. Schools around the world shut down in a matter of weeks. This unprecedented move exposed our utter reliance on brick-and-mortar schooling to meet students' and families' basic needs for education, transportation, before and after school supervision, health care, nutrition, social-emotional support, and more.

Suddenly, faced with no place to go physically, educators and the communities they serve had to rethink and react in ways requiring ingenuity, agility, and flexibility. This is one of the rare times in modern history that education has changed in such an immediate, abrupt, and dramatic fashion. Although history reveals a myriad of changes to education over the decades, the pandemic's effects were instantaneous.

If we view this as one enormous, interconnected new initiative, we have the once-in-a-lifetime chance to reconstruct a system that reflects contemporary society and educates young people accordingly. Part of this process is pruning out archaic practices and letting go of outdated beliefs about who and what public education is for.

THREE ORDERS OF BARRIERS TO CHANGE

Recalling the three orders of barriers to change, leaders must put the right elements in place to create this new world order of public education. First-order barriers may be initially the most intense to overcome, especially in communities that lack resources such as high-speed internet and 1:1 devices, much less access to regular meals and parental supervision. Providing both the technology and training on those devices for teachers and students is also a potential stumbling block to tackle. Second-order barriers, however, may be diminished in this state of emergency—educators simply don't have the option of being philosophically opposed or resistant to delivering instruction virtually. When doing business the usual way becomes substantially impossible, they will either get on board and adapt or decide to leave the profession. The third-order institutional barriers previously in place have largely already been dismantled as well—state and national assessments have been temporarily waived, bells stopped ringing, buses sat idle, sports and activities ceased, and expectations for seat time turned upside down.

What we want to avoid when addressing these barriers is applying past schema and archetypes to our blueprint for the future. Returning back to the 180-day school year, six disparate fifty-minute periods, 8 a.m.–3 p.m. structure simply won't work. The main challenge we collectively face is driving ourselves to exhaustion tending to the current environment while simultaneously harnessing a creative and imaginative energy for what could be. It's concurrently operating at the bottom (basic needs) and top (self-actualization) of Maslow's (1943, 1971) hierarchy of needs. While our immediate action is to provide safety and security for our families and communities, when that window of time passes, we will have been remiss to not have intentionally set up the new paradigms for students and teachers to go back to school.

The foundations of education in the early 20th century were revolutionary by transforming society and the trajectory of America's future. Truly innovative minds envisioned a literate populace equipped to face the demands of the industrial age that would propel the country to the most powerful and prosperous in the 20th century world. The concept of offering free public education ushered in an overwhelming commitment to civic participation, social mobility, and economic growth. We now stand on a similar historical precipice. The landscape has shifted under our feet, and it's time to learn to walk on that new terrain. We have to brave the question of what we're asking of our students that we ourselves are unwilling to risk.

Once we identify and agree on the values that the postmodern system will embody in conjunction with the purpose for their existence, education leaders need to develop a roadmap to get to those outcomes. The ten-stage new initiative implementation process encompasses the key questions, outreach processes, data collection, course adjustments, and implementation steps to guide a school or district through the monumental shifts ahead. The journey is the destination, so to speak. When we get *there*, earlier targets will eventually transition into other goals and we'll keep evolving as individuals and organizations.

Whatever comes our way, from Mother Nature to human inventiveness, a solid vetting procedure will help us navigate and build the system our students need and deserve. Much like the pioneers before us, we are setting a course for a future we can't ourselves quite imagine. But as the process unfolds, the vision becomes clearer. When the mediocre ideas fall by the wayside, only then can we realize what is the best for our students, educators, families, and communities. This is a leadership opportunity for everyone who profoundly cares about education to contribute to and participate in its metamorphosis. When we all work together on a common vision, what emerges can be truly magnificent.

EPILOGUE ACTION PLAN: CHECKLIST AND REPRODUCIBLE

The following checklist and reproducible help you apply what you learned in this epilogue and wrap up all ten stages of the initiative implementation process.

- ☐ Celebrate accomplishments with your team members!
- ☐ Add checkpoints to your calendar to send out regular reminders, updates, and messages on the initiative's progress, achievements, and impacts on student learning.
- ☐ Use the "Initiative Implementation Process: Guidance Document" reproducible (page 160) as a template to help you with school board presentations or public statements on the implementation's life cycle.

Initiative Implementation Process: Guidance Document

Directions: At the end of each chapter, you received action steps and reproducibles to use in your new initiative implementation process. All the distinct actions are compiled in the chart to illustrate the entire process. Whether you prefer to engage in the process chapter by chapter or use the following overview as a guidance document for your team, this ten-stage process is intended to help you attain your school or district's goals.

Stages	Action Planning	Notes or Evidence
Introduction	☐ Define your new initiative in a few sentences (elevator pitch). ☐ Determine whether it is externally or internally initiated and how that may affect your approach. ☐ Examine and call out the three barrier levels that may exist in your school or district related to this implementation.	
Stage 1: Research and Vet the Idea	☐ Carefully select your leadership team members. ☐ Intentionally embed the seven effective leadership practices in your team training. ☐ Complete the six steps in the research and vetting process using the "Initiative Vetting Notetaking Tool" reproducible (page 19).	
Stage 2: Pitch the Proposal	☐ Conduct the tuning protocol (see figure 2.1, page 22). ☐ Complete the "Protocol-Planning Template" reproducible (page 34). ☐ Follow up on the suggestions offered at the end of the "Protocol-Planning Template" reproducible.	
Stage 3: Determine Priorities	☐ Complete the "Initiative Prioritization Rubric" reproducible (page 52). ☐ Complete the "District Plans Crosswalk" reproducible (page 55). ☐ Use the "Cost-Benefit Analysis" reproducible (page 56) to develop and complete a cost-to-impact matrix for pending initiatives (see figures 3.4 and 3.5, page 50, as models).	

REPRODUCIBLE

Stages	Action Planning	Notes or Evidence
Stage 4: Design the Proof of Concept, Prototype, and Pilot	☐ Design the proof of concept, prototype, and pilot framework (see figure 4.1, page 58). ☐ Complete the "Four Critical Questions for the Pilot" reproducible (page 66). ☐ Complete the "Mid-Pilot Process Check" reproducible (page 67).	
Stage 5: Build Stakeholder Engagement	☐ Define your stakeholder groups by completing the "Stakeholder Groups" reproducible (page 80). ☐ Plan multi-pronged outreach strategies. ☐ Test Maslow's hierarchy of needs against your chosen engagement strategies using the "Maslow's Hierarchy of Needs Analysis" reproducible (page 83).	
Stage 6: Gather and Analyze Data	☐ Review components for survey design and focus groups, and then design your own using the "Survey Mapping Tool" and "Focus Group Mapping Tool" reproducibles (pages 97–98). ☐ Determine which passive data sources may supplement your research goals (see figure 6.3, page 94). ☐ Complete the "Data Analysis Form" reproducible (page 99).	
Stage 7: Make a Decision	☐ During the leader's presentation, use the "Questions and Commitments Notetaking Tool" reproducible (page 110) to note any questions or concerns. See the completed sample in figure 7.1 (page 104). ☐ After the presentation, have each team member complete the "Decision-Making Rubric" and "Team Decision-Making Assessment" reproducibles (pages 111–112). ☐ Review the "Criteria for Green-Lighting, Yellow-Lighting, or Red-Lighting an Initiative" reproducible (page 114), and craft specific definitions to your own initiative.	

Leading the Launch © 2022 Solution Tree Press • SolutionTree.com
Visit **go.SolutionTree.com/leadership** to download this page.

Stages	Action Planning	Notes or Evidence
Stage 8: Plan and Deliver Professional Development	☐ Map out your long-term plan for cohesive, differentiated, and ongoing professional development in the first six months of implementation (see figure 8.2, page 122). ☐ Plan for your initiative's professional development experiences using the "Professional Development Design Worksheet" reproducible (page 125). ☐ Use the "Agenda-Planning Form" reproducible (page 128) to ensure the three Rs (relevance, rigor, and relationships) are well-balanced and attended to, as demonstrated in figure 8.1 (page 120).	
Stage 9: Implement the Initiative	☐ Complete and apply the "Self-Assessment and Rating Scale Continuum" reproducible (page 140) to the initiative during the early part of this stage. ☐ When conducting observations of the implementation in action, adapt the "Implementation Observation Tool" reproducible (page 141) to fit your particular circumstances. ☐ Use the "Stakeholder Representative Assignments" reproducible (page 142) to assign tasks to stakeholders (see figure 9.2, page 137, for an example).	
Stage 10: Provide Ongoing Support	☐ Use the "Steering Guide for Monitoring Progress" reproducible (page 153) to flesh out the details for your short-term, mid-term, and long-term initiative implementation plans. ☐ Use the "Initiative Assessment Tool" reproducible (page 154) to evaluate your existing initiatives to ascertain whether they should remain in play or be eliminated in the future.	

References and Resources

ACT. (2018). *The condition of college and career readiness.* Accessed at www.act.org/content/dam/act/unsecured/documents/cccr2018/National-CCCR-2018.pdf on April 24, 2021.

Balas, E. A., & Boren, S. A. (2000). Managing clinical knowledge for health care improvement. In J. Bemmel & A. T. McCray (Eds.), *Yearbook of medical informatics 2000: Patient-centered systems* (pp. 65–70). Stuttgart, Germany: Schattauer Verlagsgesellschaft.

Bates, K., Parker, C. S., & Ogden, C. (2018, July 11). *Power dynamics: The hidden element to effective meetings.* Accessed at https://interactioninstitute.org/power-dynamics-the-hidden-element-to-effective-meetings on January 4, 2021.

Blythe, T., Allen, D., & Powell, B. S. (1999). *Looking together at student work: A companion guide to assessing student learning.* New York: Teachers College Press.

Boogren, T. H. (2018). *Take time for you: Self-care action plans for educators.* Bloomington, IN: Solution Tree Press.

BrainyQuote. (n.d.). *Albert Einstein quotes.* Accessed at www.brainyquote.com/quotes/albert_einstein_385842 on May 20, 2021.

Brown, T., & Wyatt, J. (2010). Design thinking for social innovation. *Stanford Social Innovation Review.* Accessed at https://ssir.org/articles/entry/design_thinking_for_social_innovation on January 4, 2021.

Chamberlain, P., Brown, C. H., & Saldana, L. (2011). Observational measure of implementation progress in community based settings: The stages of implementation completion (SIC). *Implementation Science, 6*(116). Accessed at https://implementationscience.biomedcentral.com/articles/10.1186/1748-5908-6-116 on May 20, 2021.

Daggett, W. R. (2015). *Rigor, relevance, and relationships in action: Innovative leadership and best practices for rapid school improvement.* Rexford, NY: International Center for Leadership in Education.

Darling-Hammond, L., Hyler, M. E., & Gardner, M. (2017). *Effective teacher professional development.* Palo Alto, CA: Learning Policy Institute.

de Brey, C., Musu, L., McFarland, J.Wilinson-Flicker, S., Diliberti, M., Zhang, A., et al. (2019). *Status and trends in the education of racial and ethnic groups 2018.* Washington, DC: National Center for Education Statistics.

Desimone, L. M., & Garet, M. (2015). Best practices in teachers' professional development in the United States. *Psychology, Society, & Education, 7*(3), 252–263.

de Vaus, D. (2014). *Surveys in social research* (6th ed.). New York: Routledge.

DiAngelo, R. (2018). *White fragility: Why it's so hard for white people to talk about racism* (Reprint ed.). Boston: Beacon Press.

DuFour, R. (2016, Summer). Loose vs. tight. *AllThingsPLC Magazine, 33.*

DuFour, R., DuFour, R., Eaker, R., Many, T. W., & Mattos, M. (2016). *Learning by doing: A handbook for Professional Learning Communities at Work* (3rd ed.). Bloomington, IN: Solution Tree Press.

Encyclopaedia Britannica. (2021). *Greta Thunberg: Swedish activist.* Accessed at www.britannica.com/biography/Greta-Thunberg on July 15, 2021.

Erkens, C., & Twadell, E. (2012). *Leading by design: An action framework for PLC at Work leaders.* Bloomington, IN: Solution Tree Press.

Ertmer, P. A. (1999). Addressing first- and second-order barriers to change: Strategies for technology integration. *Educational Technology Research and Development, 47*(4), 47–61.

Ertmer, P. A. (2005). Teacher pedagogical beliefs: The final frontier in our quest for technology integration? *Educational Technology Research and Development, 53*(4), 25–39. Accessed at https://link.springer.com/content/pdf/10.1007/BF02504683.pdf on April 26, 2021.

Fixsen, D. L., Blase, K. A., Metz, A., & Van Dyke, M. (2013). Statewide implementation of evidence-based programs. *Exceptional Children* (Special Issue), *79*(2), 213–230.

Fixsen, D. L., Blase, K. A., Timbers, G. D., & Wolf, M. M. (2001). In search of program implementation: 792 replications of the Teaching-Family Model. In G. A. Bernfeld, D. P. Farrington, & A. W. Leschied (Eds.), *Offender rehabilitation in practice: Implementing and evaluating effective programs* (pp. 149–166). London, England: Wiley.

Frontier, T., & Rickabaugh, J. (2014). *Five levers to improve learning: How to prioritize for powerful results in your school.* Alexandria, VA: Association for Supervision and Curriculum Development.

Gardner, H. (1983). *Frames of mind: The theory of multiple intelligences.* New York: Basic Books.

Green, L. W. (2008). Making research relevant: If it is an evidence-based practice, where's the practice-based evidence? *Family Practice, 25,* 20–24.

Hargie, O. (2011). *Skilled interpersonal communication: Research, theory and practice* (5th ed.). New York: Routledge.

Housel, D. A. (2020). When co-occurring factors impact adult learners: Suggestions for instruction, preservice training, and professional development. *Adult Learning, 31*(1), 6–16. Accessed at https://journals.sagepub.com/doi/pdf/10.1177/1045159519849910 on April 26, 2021.

InPraxis Group. (2006). *Effective professional development: What the research says.* Minister of Education. Alberta Education, School Improvement Branch. Accessed at https://files.eric.ed.gov/fulltext/ED494706.pdf on April 26, 2021.

Jackson, K. R., Fixsen, D., & Ward, C. (2018). *Four domains for rapid school improvement: An implementation framework.* Chapel Hill, NC: National Implementation Research Network.

Jackson, R. R. (2013). *Never underestimate your teachers: Instructional leadership for excellence in every classroom.* Alexandria, VA: Association for Supervision and Curriculum Development.

Kamberelis, G., & Dimitriadis, G. (2013). *Focus groups: From structured interviews to collective conversations.* New York: Routledge.

Lexico. (n.d.). *Implement.* Accessed at www.lexico.com/en/definition/implement on April 16, 2021.

Lor, R. R. (2017, May). *Design thinking in education: A critical review of literature.* Asian Conference on Education and Psychology (ACEP). Accessed at http://digitalknowledge.cput.ac.za/bitstream/11189/7810/1/Design%20thinking%20in%20education_%20A%20critical%20review%20of%20literature.pdf on April 26, 2021.

Lyon, A. R. (2017). *Implementation science and practice in the education sector.* Rockville, MD: Substance Abuse and Mental Health Services Administration.

Maslow, A. H. (1943). A theory of human motivation. *Psychological Review, 50*(4), 370–396.

Maslow, A. H. (1954). *Motivation and personality.* New York: Harper & Row.

Maslow, A. H. (1971). *The farther reaches of human nature.* New York: Viking Press.

McDonald, J., & Allen, D. (2021). Tuning protocol. *School Reform Initiative.* Accessed at www.schoolreforminitiative.org/download/tuning-protocol on August 10, 2021.

McDonald, J., Mohr, N., Dichter, A., & McDonald, E. C. (2013). *The power of protocols: An educator's guide to better practice* (3rd ed.). New York: Teachers College Press.

More, T. (1972). *Utopia* (P. Turner, Trans.). Baltimore: Penguin Books.

National Center for Education Statistics (NCES). (2021a, May). *English language learners in public schools.* Accessed at https://nces.ed.gov/programs/coe/indicator_cgf.asp on April 24, 2021.

National Center for Education Statistics (NCES). (2021b, May). *Students with disabilities.* Accessed at https://nces.ed.gov/programs/coe/indicator_cgg.asp on April 24, 2021.

National Implementation Research Network. (n.d.). *Module 4: Implementation stages—Topic 6—Full implementation.* Accessed at https://nirn.fpg.unc.edu/module-4/topic-6-full-implementation on January 4, 2021.

NGSS Lead States. (2013). *Read the standards.* Washington, DC: The National Academies Press. Accessed at www.nextgenscience.org/search-standards on July 15, 2021.

Onwuegbuzie, A. J., Dickinson, W. B., Leech, N. L., & Zoran, A. G. (2009). A qualitative framework for collecting and analyzing data in focus group research. *International Journal of Qualitative Methods, 8*(3), 1–21.

Rauth, I., Köppen, E., Jobst, B., & Meinel, C. (2010, November–December). *Design thinking: An educational model towards creative confidence* in Proceedings of the 1st International Conference on Design Creativity (ICDC2010), Kobe, Japan. Accessed at https://hpi.de/fileadmin/user_upload/fachgebiete/meinel/papers/Design_Thinking/2010_Rauth_ICDC.pdf on June 1, 2021.

Ritchie, H., Ortiz-Ospina, E., Beltekian, D., Mathieu, E., Hasell, J., Macdonald, B. et al. (2021, April). *COVID-19: School and workplace closures.* Accessed at https://ourworldindata.org/covid-school-workplace-closures on April 26, 2021.

Saaty, T. L., & Peniwati, K. (2013). *Group decision making: Drawing out and reconciling differences.* Pittsburgh, PA: RWS Publications.

Schmoker, M. (2004). Learning communities at the crossroads: Toward the best schools we've ever had. *Phi Delta Kappan, 86*(1), 84–88.

Sinek, S. (2011). *Start with why: How great leaders inspire everyone to take action.* New York: Portfolio.

Solution Tree. (2009, October 9). *Rick DuFour on groups vs. teams* [Video file]. Accessed at www.youtube.com/watch?v=0hV65KIItlE on January 4, 2021.

Sterman, J. D. (2006). Learning from evidence in a complex world. *American Journal of Public Health, 96*(3), 505–514.

Svensson, J., Tomson, K., & Rindzeviciute, E. (2017). Policy change as institutional work: Introducing cultural and creative industries into cultural policy. *Qualitative Research in Organizations and Management: An International Journal, 12*(2), 149–168.

Tran, H., Smith, D. A., & Buckman, D. G. (Eds.). (2020). *Stakeholder engagement: Improving education through multilevel community relations.* Lanham, MD: Rowman & Littlefield.

United States Department of Education. (2004). *Title I—Improving the academic achievement of the disadvantaged.* Accessed at www2.ed.gov/policy/elsec/leg/esea02/pg1.html on April 24, 2021.

Wallace, K. (2012). *Teachers and technology barriers: Identifying uses, barriers, and strategies to support classroom integration.* Davis, CA: ProQuest Dissertations Publishing.

Index

A

ability grouping, 151
accountability, 130–133
achievement gap, 44–46
acronyms, 87
action plan checklists and reproducibles
    building stakeholder engagement, 79–84
    designing proof of concept, 65–67
    determining priorities, 51–56
    developing and pitching a proposal, 33–35
    gathering and analyzing data, 96–99
    implementation, 139–142
    introduction, 8
    making a decision, 109–114
    professional development, 124–128
    providing ongoing support, 152–154
    researching and vetting ideas, 18–19
administering, 86, 88
adult learning theory, 115, 117
agenda design, 120
Agenda-Planning Form, 124, 128
Alberta, Canada's Ministry of Education, 121
alignment
    instructional materials and methodologies, 42
    systems, 10
analysis, 86, 89
anticipating impact on and reaction of stakeholders, 12, 16–17
assessing consensus in focus groups, 93
assessment, 130–133
    issues with, 151
assistance and support, 148–149

B

barriers to implementation, 5–8
    first-order, 5–6
    overcoming, 150–151, 157–158
    second-order, 5–6
    third-order, 7
Bates, K., 77
belonging needs, 73–74, 76, 83
Black Lives Matter, 16
blueprint for action
    pilot, 58, 60–64
    proof of concept, 58–69
    prototype, 58–62
brainstorming estimated costs, 12, 17
Brown, T., 59
building coherence and clarity, 10
building stakeholder engagement. See stakeholders
building the plane while flying it, 157

C

capacity building, 42
case studies, 8
    building stakeholder engagement, 75–76
    focus groups, 93
    implementation, 131–133
    making a decision, 104–108
    pilot, 62–63
    prototype, 59–61

providing ongoing support, 145–148
  surveys, 89–90
celebrating successes, 49, 156, 159
checklists. See action plan checklists and reproducibles
circles of influence, 70
coaching, 116–117, 126, 145
collaboration, 10
  decision making, 108
  pilot, 62–64
  professional development, 115, 117
  prototype, 59–60
commitment to accountability, 11
Common Core State Standards, 94
  initiative overload, 37–39
common goals, 11
communicating
  professional development plans, 7, 115–116
  with stakeholders, 71–72
connection to other initiatives, 39, 42–43
consulting teams, 22
costs and resources, 40, 49–51
  brainstorming estimates, 12, 17–18
COVID-19 pandemic, 135–138, 157
Criteria for Green-Lighting, Yellow-Lighting, or Red-Lighting an Initiative, 109, 114
criteria for preventing initiative overload,
  connection to other initiatives, 39, 42–43
  costs and resources, 49–51
  discipline policy cost-benefit analysis, 50, 56
  equity, 39, 44–46
  impact on learning, 39, 43–44
  initiative prioritization rubric, 39–40, 52–54
  required service, 40, 48
  sample district plans crosswalk, 41–42, 55
  strategic alignment, 40–42
  support from stakeholders, 40, 46–47
  timing and readiness, 40, 47–48
culturally responsive leadership, 122
culture of continued growth, 144–148
curriculum development, 42

D

Daggett, W., 115–118
damage control, 135–136
Darling-Hammond, L., 115–117

Data Analysis Form, 96, 99
data compilation methods, 94–96
data needs and passive sources, 94–95
Decision-Making Rubric, 109, 111
demographics, 14
designing prototypes. See prototypes
designing surveys. See surveys
design thinking
  defined, 58
  proof of concept through, 58–59
Desimone, L., 119
determining priorities, 4, 7
  action plan, 51–56
  cost-to-impact matrix, 50
  criteria for preventing initiative overload, 39–51
  discipline policy cost-benefit analysis, 50, 56
  initiative overload, 37–39
  initiative prioritization rubric, 39–40, 52–54
  managing multiple implementations, 38
  sample district plans crosswalk, 41–42, 55
de Vaus, D., 85–86
developing and pitching a proposal, 4, 7
  action plan, 33–35
  real-world scenarios, 24–32
  tuning protocol, 21–24
developing awareness and alignment, 12, 14
developing leadership capacity, 11
diffusion, 3
Dimitriadis, G., 91
disciplinary issues, 151
discipline policy cost-benefit analysis, 50, 56
dissemination, 3
districtwide joint memo on PLCs, 147–148
DuFour, Rebecca, 11
DuFour, Richard, 11, 145

E

Eaker, R., 11
educational jargon, 87
effective leadership practices, 10
Einstein, A., 15
elevator pitch, 8, 160
eliminating ineffective and outdated programs, 7
engagement
  defined, 64
  negative, 103

stakeholder, 64–84
student, 42
English learners, 44–45, 151
equity, 1, 151
determining priorities, 40, 44–46
Erkens, C., 10
Ertmer, P., 5–6
esteem needs, 73–74, 76, 83

F

facilitating shared responsibility, 10
feedback
considering all, 64
from students, 77
implementation, 129
negative engagement, 103
professional development, 116–117, 127
seeking from stakeholders, 4
systems, 42
first-order barriers, 5–7
defined, 6
overcoming, 150–151, 157
Fixsen, D., 143
"flavor of the month," 2, 147
Focus Group Mapping Tool, 91, 96, 98
focus groups
case study, 93–94
intended results, 91–92
location, 91
moderator, 91–92
participants, 91–92
forecasting the future, 12, 15–16
Four Critical Questions for the Pilot, 52, 65–66
Frontier, T., 38–39
funding sources, 16–17

G

Gardner, M., 115
Garet, M., 119
gathering and analyzing data, 4, 7, 85–86
action plan, 96–99
data needs and passive sources, 94–95
focus groups, 91–94
supplemental data complication methods, 94–96
surveys, 86–91
gender equality, 16
go slow to go fast, 3
Google Apps for Education, 106–107

green-lighting an initiative, 102, 156

H

Hargie, O., 71, 90
Housel, D. A., 117
humor, 119–120
Hyler, M., 115

I

identifying the rationale, 12–13
IDEO, 59
impact on learning, 39, 43–44
implementation, 2, 4, 7, 129–130
action plans, 139–142, 159–162
assessment and accountability, 130–133
barriers to, 5–7
case study, 131–133
defined, 2–3
moving forward, 135–138
orders of barriers to change, 157–158
stages of, 155–157
stakeholder representative assignments, 137–138, 142
ten stages, 4
three scenarios, 133–135
wellness center observation tool, 132–133
Implementation Observation Tool, 139, 141
Individuals with Disabilities Education Act (IDEA), 45
Initiative Assessment Tool, 152, 154
Initiative Implementation Process: Guidance Document, 159–162
initiative overload, 37–39
action plan, 51–56
cost-to-impact matrix, 50
criteria for preventing, 39–51
discipline policy cost-benefit analysis, 50, 56
initiative prioritization rubric, 39–40, 52–54
managing multiple implementations, 38
sample district plans crosswalk, 41–42, 55
Initiative Prioritization Rubric, 39–40, 52–54
Initiative Vetting Notetaking Tool, 19, 23
instructional issues, 151

J

Jackson, K. R., 143, 146
Jackson, R. R., 6
job-embedded content, 115, 117, 126

K

Kamberelis, G., 91

L

leadership, 156
   development, 42
   teams, 11–12
Leading by Design (Erkens & Twadell), 10
legal mandates, 5
levers, 38–39
Lor, R. R., 58–59
Lyon, A. R., 2, 130

M

making a decision, 4, 7
   action plan, 109–114
   art and science of, 108
   case study, 104–108
   green-, yellow-, or red-lighting, 101–108
   parent letter for Google Apps for Education implementation, 106–107
   Questions and Commitments Notetaking Tool, 104–106, 110
   sharing with stakeholders, 64
managing multiple implementations, 38
Many, T. W., 11
Maslow, A., 73–75, 83–84, 91, 158
Maslow's hierarchy of needs, 73–75, 83–84, 91, 158
   analysis form, 79, 83–84
   strategies for family and community engagement, 74–75
Mattos, M., 11
McDonald, J., 21
memorandum of understanding (MOU), 104, 146–148
Mid-Pilot Process Check, 63–64, 65, 67
modeling
   practices and expectations, 10
   professional development, 115, 126
More, T., 1

N

National Center for Education Statistics (NCES), 45
National Implementation Research Network, 130
Next Generation Science Standards (NGSS), 16–17, 25–27

O

Office of Civil Rights, 48
Ogden, C., 77
organizational issues, 151
Our World in Data, 136

P

parents, 70
   involving, 42
   sample letter to, 106–107
Parker, C., 77
Peniwati, K., 103
physiological needs, 73, 75–76, 84
piloting an initiative, 4
   case study, 62–63
   defined, 58
   implementation, 155–156
   mid-pilot process check, 63–64
   sample plan, 60–61
pitching proposals. See developing and pitching a proposal
planning for outreach, 72–75
positive behavior intervention and supports (PBIS), 49
poverty, 45
power dynamics, 77–78
primary stakeholders, 70, 81–82
prioritizing. See determining priorities
processes, 8
professional development
   action plan, 124–128
   agenda design, 120
   communication of, 7
   culture of continued growth, 144–148
   determining priorities, 42
   key features, 115–117
   planning and delivering, 4, 7
   relationships, 117, 119–120, 124, 128
   relevance, 117–119, 124, 128
   research base for, 117
   rigor, 117–118, 124, 128
   sample district leadership and action steps, 122–123
   sustained delivery, 120–121
Professional Development Design Worksheet, 120, 124–127

professional learning community (PLC)
    case study, 145–148
    critical questions, 43–44, 62, 118
    proof of concept through design thinking, 58–59
    defined, 68
Protocol-Planning Template, 34–35
prototype, 4, 58–62
    case study, 59–60
    defined, 58
    extending the phase, 102
    implementation, 155–156
providing ongoing support, 4, 7, 143–144
    action plan, 152–154
    assistance and support, 148–149
    case study, 145–148
    culture of continued growth, 144–148
    districtwide joint memo on PLCs, 147–148
    providing ongoing support, 145–148
    unproductive practices, 149–152

Q

questions
    focus groups, 91–92
    for the pilot, 65–66
    making a decision, 104–106
    Maslow's hierarchy of needs, 83–84
    open-ended, 88–89
    preventing initiative overload, 39–40
    providing ongoing support, 154
    stakeholder groups, 81
    tuning protocols, 23–24, 28
Questions and Commitments Notetaking Tool, 101, 104–106, 109–110

R

red-lighting an initiative, 103, 156
reducing biased outcomes, 4
reducing redundancies, 150
reflection
    implementation, 134
    leadership effectiveness, 11
    professional development, 116–117, 127
relationships
    collaborative, 10
    professional development, 115, 117, 119–120, 124, 128
relevance, 115, 117–119, 124–128

religious minorities, 48
reproducibles. See action plan checklists and reproducibles
required service, 40, 48
research, 86–87
    base for professional development, 117
researching and vetting ideas, 4, 7, 9–11, 155
    leadership team, 11–12
    six steps for vetting, 12–18
    action plan, 18–19
Rickabaugh, J., 38–39
rigor, 115, 118, 124, 128

S

Saaty, T. L., 103
safety needs, 73–76, 84
sample district leadership professional development and action steps, 122–123
sample district plans crosswalk, 41–42, 55
sample workshop agenda, 120
Schmoker, M., 116
school climate and culture, 42
secondary stakeholders, 70, 81–82
second-order barriers, 5–7
    defined, 6
    overcoming, 150–151, 157
self-actualization needs, 73–74, 76, 83
Self-Assessment and Rating Scale Continuum, 139–140
Sinek, S., 13
skill
    defined, 6
    or will, 6
slang, 87
social justice, 1
social-emotional learning, 42–43
stages of implementation, 8, 155–157
Stakeholder Groups, 79–82
Stakeholder Representative Assignments, 137–138, 142
stakeholders
    action plan, 79–84
    anticipating impact on and reaction of, 12, 16–17
    building engagement, 4, 7, 64–65
    building engagement, 64–65

case study, 75–76
circles of influence, 70
communicating with, 71–72
groups, 69–71, 80–82
making a decision, 104–106
Maslow's hierarchy of needs, 73–75, 83–84
one size does not fit all, 75–78
plan for outreach, 72–75
representative assignments, 137–138, 142
seeking feedback from, 4, 7
soliciting support from, 40, 46–47
STEAM and STEM opportunities, 3, 25–27
steering, 148–149, 152–153
Steering Guide for Monitoring Progress, 148, 153
STEM programs, 48
steps for vetting an idea
anticipate impact on and reaction of stakeholders, 12, 16–17
brainstorm estimated costs, 12, 17–18
develop awareness and alignment, 12, 14
forecast the future, 12, 15–16
identify the rationale, 12–13
tap into history and background, 12, 15
strategic alignment, 39–42
stratification, 151
student engagement, 42
student learning and feedback systems, 42
student transitions to higher education and careers, 42
students with special needs, 16, 151
Survey Mapping Tool, 96–97
surveys
administration, 86, 88
analysis, 86, 89
case study, 89–97
design, 86–88
implementation, 133–134
research, 86–87
Surveys in Social Research (de Vaus), 85–86
systemic racism, 45

T

tapping into history and background, 12, 15
Team Decision-Making Assessment, 109, 112–113
technical terms, 87
technology support, 42
ten stages of the initiative implementation process, 4
tertiary stakeholders, 70, 80–82
testing proof of concept, 4, 7, 57
blueprint for action, 58–64
third-order barriers, 7
overcoming, 150–151, 157–158
Thunberg, G., 16
timing and readiness, 40, 47–48
traditions, 151
tuning protocol, 21–24
clarifying questions, 23–24, 28
examples, 24–32
sample, 22–23
Twadell, E., 10
2011 Fair, Accurate, Inclusive, and Respectful (FAIR) Education Act, 5

U

unproductive practices, 149–152
Utopia (More), 1

W

Ward, C., 143
wellness center observation tool, 132–133
will or skill, 6

Y

yellow-lighting an initiative, 102, 156

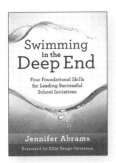

Swimming in the Deep End
Jennifer Abrams
Acquire the knowledge and resources necessary to lead successful change initiatives in schools. In *Swimming in the Deep End*, author Jennifer Abrams dives deep into the four foundational skills required of effective leadership and provides ample guidance for cultivating each.
BKF830

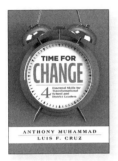

Time for Change
Anthony Muhammad and Luis F. Cruz
Exceptional leaders have four distinctive skills: strong communication, the ability to build trust, the ability to increase the skills of those they lead, and a results orientation. *Time for Change* offers powerful guidance for those seeking to develop and strengthen these skills.
BKF683

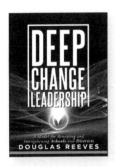

Deep Change Leadership
Douglas Reeves
As 21st century educators grapple with unprecedented challenges, schools and districts require a model of change leadership that responds to shifting environmental realities. In *Deep Change Leadership*, author Douglas Reeves offers up a pragmatic model that embraces engagement, inquiry, and focused action.
BKF935

Small Changes, Big Impact
Anthony R. Reibel and Matt Thede
Discover a pathway to improvement that is simple and field tested. Designed as a practical guide to school reform, this resource outlines a series of ten small-scale changes powerful enough to make a lasting impact in schools and districts.
BKF921

Visit SolutionTree.com or call 800.733.6786 to order.

Wait! Your professional development journey doesn't have to end with the last pages of this book.

We realize improving student learning doesn't happen overnight. And your school or district shouldn't be left to puzzle out all the details of this process alone.

No matter where you are on the journey, we're committed to helping you get to the next stage.

Take advantage of everything from **custom workshops** to **keynote presentations** and **interactive web and video conferencing**. We can even help you develop an action plan tailored to fit your specific needs.

Let's get the conversation started.

Call 888.763.9045 today.

SolutionTree.com